Multi-Sensory Worship

MULTI-SENSORY WORSHIP

Scripture Union, 207–209 Queensway, Bletchley, MK2 2EB, UK
email: info@scriptureunion.org.uk
www.scriptureunion.org.uk

Scripture Union Australia: Locked Bag 2, Central Coast Business Centre, NSW 2252
www.su.org.au

ISBN 978 1 84427 397 3
First published in Great Britain by Scripture Union 2009
Copyright © Sue Wallace

British Library Cataloguing-in-Publication data: a catalogue record for this book is available from the British Library.

Cover design by waldonwhitejones of Basildon, Essex, UK

Photographs by Sue Wallace

Editing and internal page design by Creative Pages: www.creativepages.co.uk

Printed and bound by Melita Press, Malta

Scripture Union is an international Christian charity working with churches in more than 130 countries providing resources to bring the good news about Jesus Christ to children, young people and families – and to encourage them to develop spiritually through the Bible and prayer. As well as coordinating a network of volunteers, staff and associates who run holidays, church-based events and school Christian groups, Scripture Union produces a wide range of publications and supports those who use their resources through training programmes.

Multi-Sensory Worship

Over 60 ready-to-use prayer activities
for creative churches

Sue Wallace

Thanks

There are many people I would like to thank:

- firstly, as ever, God, the Three in One, who constantly inspires us all;

- next, the Visions community, for releasing me to spend time writing;

- my other half, Malcolm, who has always been able to spot the practical flaws in a great idea, and fix them;

- the Dean and chapter of York Minster for letting us use their building;

- canons Jeremy Fletcher and Glyn Webster who have been helping us learn how to blend creative prayer ideas with inspiring liturgy;

- the CJ (IBVM) nuns who got me praying creatively with the Bible when I was young;

- Father Bede for inspiring Visions anew with insights into community, scripture and prayer;

- Father Stephen for teaching us how the Orthodox pray;

- Bishop Graham Cray for getting us started back in 1991;

- all the 'emerging church' people who have supported us so much in the past, especially COTA in Seattle for their lovely hospitality;

- members of the Fresh Expressions committees who are doing so much good work;

- Roger Simpson and the staff of St Michael le Belfrey for their continued prayer and practical support, and all the great staff and students on the NOC (YMC) ordination course who have been so supportive;

- and special thanks to the people I'm sure I've forgotten to whom I owe so much!

Contents

Index of Bible verses

Index of Christian feasts and themes

Index of types of prayer

Introduction

This and other books in this series all began in the Visions community in York when we realised how pitifully bad we were at praying. Visions started in 1989 out of a mission in the city, and grew into an alternative and experimental worship group. Over the years, we have taken our inspiration from many places: from Anglican prayer groups, the Iona community, Orthodox churches, Catholic monasteries, charismatic conferences, emerging churches and parts of the 'Fresh Expressions' movement around the world. Along the way we have learned a great deal; that different prayer and worship activities suit different personalities, for example, and that being physically engaged in an activity helps spiritual truths sink in.

Since the *Multi-Sensory* books began to appear, it has been exciting to see many different churches, groups and individuals trying new prayer and worship ideas, and new alternative worship communities coming into being. It has been particularly encouraging to see people being creative and flexible with the ideas, adapting and changing them to suit their own circumstances. Yet, most exciting of all has been meeting people from time to time at conferences and hearing the story of someone coming to faith as a result of a prayer activity!

Over the years, Visions has changed. One development is that once a month we team up with York Minster and do a large service called Transcendence. This has meant that we have had the whole new – wonderful! – problem of scaling up prayer and worship ideas from the setting of an intimate group to use with a congregation of around 100. This latest book is born out of those experiences.

My prayer is that this collection of ideas and activities will inspire you to more creative worship in your church and small group communities.

Preparing your building and environment for prayer

A prayerful environment is really conducive to meaningful worship, so spend time preparing the space you have. Make your building as comfortable and welcoming as possible. While you might use rugs, beanbags and cushions in a small group setting, it may be more difficult to achieve that in a large church building. Remember, anyway, that not everyone is physically able to sit on the floor. But subdued lighting, incense or candles and gentle background music often help set the scene and prepare people to meet God in prayer. Images projected onto walls and swathes of material draped around the walls can also make your hall less spartan and functional. If your church building is blessed with beautiful stained glass windows or paintings, draw attention to them with spotlights or by rearranging the seating.

Remember to be safe. If you choose to use candles, always position them carefully. It does no harm to have a bucket of sand or a fire extinguisher nearby. If you use electrical or electronic equipment, check that the cabling is safely anchored out of the way of people traffic.

Different prayer ideas will suit different personalities. One person, for example, may find a particular ritual deeply helpful, whereas another may be unable to take part, either because at that time it may be too painful, or because it makes them feel uncomfortable. For this reason, it is important to make it clear that people are free to opt out or just watch if they wish.

It may also be that some members of your congregation feel a little wary or suspicious of different kinds of prayer and worship activities. Always give them the option of observing rather than participating, and make sure that they are comfortable with what is happening.

If the activity includes writing something, be sure to let people know if their writing is going to be seen by anyone else as this will save misunderstanding and embarrassment. If no one else is going to see their contribution, people can be free to write some personal things. But if the writing is to be placed on display in some way, they will be more likely to write things that other people can understand and respond with their 'Amen.'

Preparing the people for prayer

Psalm 46:10 says, "Be still and know that I am God." It's helpful to begin any time of worship with a 'stilling' prayer exercise, helping people focus on God and getting rid of some of the distractions of the day. A number of these 'breathing prayers' can be found in *Multi-Sensory Prayer.*

Sue Wallace

1 Washing at the pool

Resources

You will need: a number of bowls filled with water; a paddling pool or font (placed, if possible, at the foot of a cross); towels, paper towels or newspaper; washable felt-tip pens; 10 cm squares of clear plastic (use discarded plastic packaging or OHP acetate); background music or song.

Method

Give out the plastic squares and pens at the start of the service or prayer meeting. Then, when you are ready, invite everyone to write on the plastic anything they want to confess to God. Reassure them that no one else is going to read what they write.

Next, play some music. This could be a song of confession which includes the words 'Lord have mercy' as part of the lyrics, or any song about washing such as 'When I went down in the river to pray.' During the music, invite people to come up and wash their pieces of plastic in the pool, placing their rinsed plastic on the towels or paper. When everyone has washed their plastic, say a prayer of assurance that God has forgiven them.

Tried & tested

We've used this prayer activity in a number of places at different times, most memorably in the chapter house of York Minster, when we created a large version of the Pool of Siloam for a service about the healing of the blind man in John 9, complete with a palm tree in the middle. It is really effective when people literally watch their sins float off the plastic and disappear!

Be sure to check in advance both the type of plastic you are using and all your pen supply! If the squares don't wash off properly it may be quite upsetting to people to see their 'sins' haven't gone away!

2 Flash of forgiveness

Resources

You will need: a metal bowl placed where it is easily seen by everyone; something safe to stand the bowl on – either the stone church floor or metal table or equivalent; some flash paper (which can be bought from conjurers' suppliers); a taper; matches; pencils; background music.

Important: Read and obey the safety instructions on the packet of flash paper carefully. Do not stand too close; do not allow children to get too close.

Method

At the start of the service, give out small pieces of flash paper and pencils. Alternatively, set up a table which people visit during the service. Invite people to write down anything about which they want to say sorry to God. Play or sing a song about forgiveness or God's mercy towards us while people are writing. Then everyone should put their paper in the metal container. Pray, thanking God for his promise of forgiveness, while someone sets light to the flash paper.

There will be a sudden fiery flash – and the papers will have completely disappeared! Encourage people to look into the empty bowl for themselves. Explain that God can take our sins away completely because of what Jesus did for us on the cross.

3 Dark places

Resources

You will need: a collection of small stones – large enough to write on, but small enough so that lots will fit into a large bowl; some OHP pens or permanent markers; a 'dark place' representing a tomb – this could be a tent covered in blackout material, or a table with dark material draped over it; a water feature to represent a fountain, or a large bowl filled with water; background music.

Method

Place the fountain or bowl of water in the centre of the worship space, where it can be easily seen. Place the dark place or 'tomb' some distance away. Put the permanent markers near the entrance to the dark place. Provide plenty of markers so that the queues to use them don't become too long.

Read the story of the raising of Lazarus from John 11 and talk about how the dead Lazarus was placed in the tomb for four days before being raised by Christ. Invite people to take a stone and to think about someone they know who is in a dark place at the moment. They are going to write their name or initials on the stone; but be sure to let them know that these names will be read by others. They could choose to write several names, or to describe a generic group, such as 'those suffering from depression.' As people are thinking about this, play some prayerful music or a song of intercession.

Invite people to come to the dark place, write the name of the group or person they are thinking of on the stone using the OHP pen and place the stone inside the dark place. Then they should take a different stone (placed inside the 'tomb' by someone else) and pray for the person or people whose names are written there. Encourage them to pray that these people will be raised from their dark place to a place of life.

Finally, after praying, they can place their stone in the water of the fountain, symbolising the never-ending living water that Christ gives, bubbling up to eternal life.

Close the activity with a prayer of thanks for the promise of resurrection and eternal life that Christ has given us.

4 Prayer patterns

(with thanks to Richard Horton for designing the pattern)

Resources

You will need: photocopies of **Prayer patterns** (page 14); several pots of colouring materials such as crayons, coloured pencils or felt-tip pens; tables to work at or boards or books to rest on.

Method

Read John 20:1–18 or Luke 24:13–34. In both these accounts, the risen Jesus isn't recognised at first, so talk about that with your group. Then invite them to colour their patterns.

While they are colouring, suggest they can pray for

• people who are sad;

- people who feel they have no hope;

- people who need some colour in their lives.

Talk about how it took a while for some of the disciples to see that they were with Jesus. They thought they were talking to a stranger. So it can take us a while to see things properly.

Ask everyone: what can you see in these patterns?

- Can you spot the cross?

- Can you find the heart?

- Can you see the fish?

When everyone has finished, put the patterns on the table as a way of giving the prayers to God. Tell everyone they can have them back later! They may wish to put their names on their paper to remind them which one is theirs.

Tried & tested

We first did this prayer activity for an all-age Easter service. After everyone had coloured their patterns and prayed, we placed the pieces of paper on the altar table to decorate it as we prepared to celebrate communion.

5 Drumming prayers 1

In recent years we have loved using percussion as part of our prayer and worship. The great thing about it is that it is very inclusive and people can take part at their own levels.

Resources

You will need: a selection of drums and percussion instruments. You can buy or borrow these, or make some of your own. If you decide to buy some, I would recommend a djembe (or African drum) or a pair of congas to lead with; some more djembes or congas if you can afford them; or alternatively darbukas which are much cheaper (shaped like djembes, made of metal). If space is an issue, you can buy flat 'shape drums' which fit more easily into church cupboards.

A large selection of musical shakers is also good to have. You can get some shaped like eggs or fruit and vegetables which have a lovely tone.

If you can't afford to buy any instruments or want to supplement bought instruments, you can use upside down buckets or bins, either plastic or metal, or empty plastic bottles from water coolers. You can also make homemade claves from short lengths of dowel.

Shakers can be made from empty film reel canisters, plastic bottles of different shapes and sizes and plastic herb and spice pots. Fill them with rice, lentils or dried peas and seal with strong tape so they don't pop open and spill their contents everywhere! Different pulses make slightly different sounds. Crisp tubes with plastic lids can also be used either as shakers or as drums depending on whether you fill them with rice or leave them empty.

> If you are unfamiliar with drums, it may help you to know that the **djembe** is a skin-covered drum shaped like a goblet, played with bare hands. The **darbuka** is a similar shape but smaller and usually played with the fingertips. The **conga** is a tall, narrow drum, usually played in a set of two with fingers and palms.

Percussion instruments are great to use with adults and children. However, if children are involved, it's wise not to give out the instruments until you are ready for them to make a noise with them – it's just too great

Prayer patterns

a temptation to have them nearby while you give them instructions! The other thing to remember when drumming with children is that it will be wise to swap around the instruments regularly to avoid arguments.

Method

If you have time, start with some 'warm-ups'. Invite people to wiggle their fingers, circle their arms in the air, rub their hands together and clap their hands. As soon as you distribute the instruments, teach some basic rules. The most important of these is that when you raise your hands in the air they have to raise their hands in the air too – and stop playing! Obviously, they cannot play their instruments with hands raised, so this is very useful when you need some silence.

Then teach everyone that when you crouch low they should play more quietly and when you stand taller they should play more loudly. Practise this, by getting them to watch you, playing quietly as you crouch low, getting more loud as you get taller and stopping when you stop. Do this a few times, varying the times they play from a short period to a longer period of time so that they learn to watch and stop on cue. When they have practised this for a while, move onto using the drums to pray with.

In Psalm 150 and 1 Chronicles 13:8 percussion instruments are described as being used to praise God. Explain that drumming can be used in prayer to help us concentrate on the person or situation being prayed for.

In small groups, encourage everyone to sit in circles so that they can all see each other. Get each person to play the rhythm of their own name in turn, for example 'Sue Wall-ace... Sue Wall-ace.' Some people will need help deciding which rhythm to play, as some names can be played in different ways. Then go around the circle again, this time inviting each person in turn to play the rhythm of their name while everyone else plays the rhythm 'God bless' and their name: 'God bless Sue Wall-ace... God bless Sue Wall-ace.' Do this four times for each name and then move onto the next name. By the time you have been all around the circle each person will have been prayed for by everyone else.

With a whole congregation you could split into smaller groups to pray for the area around the church, using the rhythm of the street names. So one group could play the rhythm 'Al-bert Square' while everyone else plays 'God bless Al-bert Square' and then another group plays 'Co-ro-nat-tion Street' while everyone else plays 'God bless Co-ro-na-tion Street.' Practise first to get the timing right. But remind everyone that it's the prayer that matters, not the musical excellence. You will find that people are very ragged at first but get better quite quickly, so you might want to do the whole activity twice so that it's more satisfying to everyone.

When you have finished the drumming prayer session, pray a summary prayer to cover all the situations you have been praying for, one that everyone can say 'Amen' to. Then have the percussion collected by volunteers so that the instruments do not disturb anyone as the service progresses.

6 Drumming prayers 2

Resources

You will need: a selection of drums and percussion instruments – bought, borrowed, or home-made; photocopies of **Drumming Prayer Music** on page 16; a backing track with rhythms on it or some musicians rehearsed to continue playing when others have stopped (optional); a piece of coloured card on which is written,

Lord Jesus, hear all our prayers,

Jesus, hear us.

Method

You could use the warm-up exercises in **Drumming prayers 1**, if you have time.

Make sure that you have taught everyone that when you raise your hands everyone else needs to raise their hands too. Then give out your percussion instruments, dividing your congregation into two groups – one group using instruments that are hit and another group using instruments that are shaken.

Invite the group using instruments that are shaken to play the rhythm 'Je-sus hear us.' When that rhythm has been nicely established, bring in the other group to play the rhythm 'Lord Je-sus, hear all our prayers.' Use the **Drumming Prayer Music** below to establish the rhythm. Invite more experienced musicians to play more complex cross rhythms over these two rhythms if they wish, when the prayers begin.

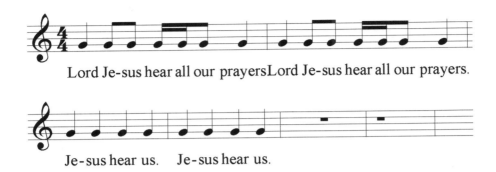

When you have practised playing the rhythms, raise your hands to stop the musicians and explain that you are going to pass around a piece of coloured card, and whoever has that card can say the name of a country or world situation that needs prayer, or even say a longer prayer if they wish, before passing the card to someone else. Ask them to end their prayer with the words, 'Lord Jesus, hear all our prayers, Jesus hear us.' During a period of drumming after this prayer, invite people to use the drums to pray for the situation that was mentioned, then raise your hands allowing the next person holding the card to pray or just say the name of a country or situation. The period of time that each drumming section lasts really depends on how many people you have to get around. It also depends on how long it takes people to relax into playing the drums instinctively. If you allow for some longer drumming periods you will find people get more confident and start to 'do their own thing' with cross-rhythms.

When everyone who wishes to has prayed, complete the session with a short spoken prayer and collect the percussion instruments.

7 Drumming the Bible

Resources
You will need: a selection of drums and percussion – bought, borrowed or home-made; a musician to help with the rhythms (optional); a headset or clip-on microphone so that people can hear what the leader is saying while drums are being played; photocopies of **Give thanks to the Lord** (page 17).

Some psalms are easier to drum with than others; a section of verses from Psalm 136 is given for you to start with. But you could choose another one, you could take some verses from the Gospels, or you could even write your own.

Method
Give out the percussion instruments. Ask the group of people who have shakers to play the simple rhythm: 'Thanks – thanks – thanks – thanks.' Then ask everyone who has a drum to play the rhythm: 'For his stead-fast love en-dures for e-ver.'

Practise both rhythms together for a while and then, when everyone seems confident, explain that we are going to drum a psalm. The shakers will keep the rhythm with their 'Thanks – thanks – thanks – thanks' rhythm while you (or a musician) lead the first line, and all the drums come in with the response 'For his stead-fast love en-dures for e-ver.' If it's going well you could invite a few more experienced musicians to drum cross-rhythms when everyone else drums the 'steadfast' response. At the end of the psalm repeat the response yourself as a cue to everyone to repeat it extra loud to finish off.

Give thanks to the Lord

– selected verses from Psalm 136

Begin by starting the shakers playing their 'thanks' rhythm.

Leader: Give thanks to the LORD, for he is good.
Drums: *For his stead-fast love en-dures for e-ver.*

Leader: Give thanks to the God of gods.
Drums: *For his stead-fast love en-dures for e-ver.*

Leader: Give thanks to the Lord of lords:
Drums: *For his stead-fast love en-dures for e-ver.*

Leader: To him who alone does great wonders,
Drums: *For his stead-fast love en-dures for e-ver.*

Leader: Who by his understanding made the heavens,
Drums: *For his stead-fast love en-dures for e-ver.*

Leader: Who spread out the earth upon the waters,
Drums: *For his stead-fast love en-dures for e-ver.*

Leader: Who made the great lights –
Drums: *For his stead-fast love en-dures for e-ver.*

Leader: The sun to govern the day,
Drums: *For his stead-fast love en-dures for e-ver.*

Leader: The moon and stars to govern the night;
Drums: *For his stead-fast love en-dures for e-ver.*

Leader: To him who led his people through the desert,
Drums: *For his stead-fast love en-dures for e-ver.*

Leader: To the One who remembered us in our low estate
Drums: *For his stead-fast love en-dures for e-ver.*

Leader: And freed us from our enemies,
Drums: *For his stead-fast love en-dures for e-ver.*

Leader: And who gives food to every creature.
Drums: *For his stead-fast love en-dures for e-ver.*

Leader: Give thanks to the God of heaven.
Drums: *For his stead-fast love en-dures for e-ver.*

Leader: Give thanks to God for he is good.
Drums: *For his stead-fast love en-dures for e-ver.*

Leader: Give thanks to God for he is good.
All: *FOR HIS STEADFAST LOVE ENDURES FOR EVER!*

8 Sad faces, happy faces

Resources

You will need: a collection of faces of world leaders – either cut from magazines and newspapers or printed from the Internet. Or alternatively you could use the faces of your congregation – taking photos of them (with permission) and printing them out. Close-up faces looking straight into the camera work better for this activity than faces in profile.

Method

Invite everyone to take a face. Make a little concertina out of the face which, when it is held up and tilted upwards and downwards will produce different expressions and will appear to change from sad to happy. Show an example of a finished face picture so people know what they are working towards, then explain how it is done.

Fold the picture backwards halfway through where each eye is in the picture and then fold the whole thing forwards as if you were just folding it in half normally where the nose is in the picture (the inner line on the first photo).

When you tilt it forwards, so that you are looking at it from the top, the face looks sad. When you tilt it the other way, so that you are looking at it from the bottom, the face looks happy.

Pass the pictures around and, as you look at each picture, tilt it from sad to happy and, as you do so, either:

- pray for each world leader, that they will follow Christ, act justly, and have joy

or:

- pray for each person pictured in your congregation, that they will experience the healing love and joy of Christ.

Tried & tested

> We first used this prayer activity at an afternoon all-age service when we had been thinking about the transforming power of Christ renewing our minds (Romans 12:1,2). The faces activity thrilled and delighted both young and old and there was a real sense of prayer as people turned their world leader's faces from sad to happy.

9 Umbrellas

Resources

You will need: a collection of umbrellas; some small whiteboards with marker pens, or blackboards and chalk or notepads and pens; rugs or cushions to place under the umbrellas; the script from page 65 or a recording of it on an MP3 or CD player.

Method

Sit people in twos or threes on rugs or cushions and give out the whiteboards or notepads, one to each group. Then one person can put up the group's umbrella. Slowly read out the script. Another person from each small group then takes the notepad or whiteboard and writes down a few things that they are scared about. They silently ask God to reassure them that he will surround and protect them, no matter how stormy life gets. When they have finished, they turn the page or wipe the board ready for the next person in the group.

Tried & tested

 You can use any umbrellas you like, although large golfing umbrellas are the most effective. It can still be difficult, though, to fit many people under an umbrella at any one time, so an alternative is to have a number of prayer stations decorated with umbrellas that people can visit. We also used an umbrella decorated with LED lights, which looked wonderful from a distance.

10 Hidden things

Resources
You will need: a collection of small cobbles – available from garden centres and useful for all sorts of different prayer activities; stickers or masking tape; felt-tip pens or pencils; background music (optional).

Method
Place a sticker or piece of tape on each stone, then turn them over so that the sticker is on the underside. Arrange them around the front of your worship space. Place the pens near the stones.

Read Matthew 10:26–31:

> So do not be afraid of them. There is nothing concealed that will not be disclosed, or hidden that will not be made known. What I tell you in the dark, speak in the daylight; what is whispered in your ear, proclaim from the roofs. Do not be afraid of those who kill the body but cannot kill the soul. Rather, be afraid of the one who can destroy both soul and body in hell. Are not two sparrows sold for a penny? Yet not one of them will fall to the ground apart from the will of your Father. And even the very hairs of your head are all numbered. So don't be afraid; you are worth more than many sparrows.

Explain that Jesus told us not to be afraid, that we are extraordinarily precious to him and that he knows about all our needs, even the hidden ones. Encourage people to write a hidden prayer need on the tape on the underside of a stone and then place it face down once more. Explain that though what is written remains anonymous, other people may read it. You could play a piece of music or a song about prayer or about God's protection while people are writing. When everyone has finished, invite everyone to turn over a few stones that are not their own and pray for those needs, then return the stones. You could finish by repeating the passage from Matthew.

Tried & tested

We have used this prayer activity in a number of different types of service. The most powerful thing about it is that people's hidden needs get prayed for, while anonymity is preserved.

11 Come follow me

Resources
You will need: a piece of carpet, some fabric or a long roll of paper to represent a road; a pair of sandals.

Method

Place the sandals at the beginning of the 'road'. Read Luke 5:1–11, which describes the calling of the first disciples to follow Jesus. Invite anyone who wishes to come up and place their shoes on the road behind Jesus' sandals, as a sign that they want to follow in Christ's footsteps, leaving a bit of space between each pair of shoes. If anyone has disabilities which mean they cannot easily take off their shoes, invite them to use another item of clothing instead, such as a scarf.

When everyone who wishes to has placed their shoes along the road, remind people that sometimes it's not easy to follow in Christ's footsteps and do things God's way. Then ask people to stand by someone else's shoes or scarf and mentally (but not literally) 'step into their shoes' and pray for that other person for a while in silence. At the end of the prayer, people can collect their shoes and return to their places.

Tried & tested

" You could use any reading about the cost of following Christ with this activity. The beauty is that it is infinitely adaptable in terms of size of group, as there are always the right numbers of shoes available! "

12 Balloons 1

Resources

You will need: a helium balloon party kit and either a balloon per person or one per family group; luggage labels – purchased or home-made from pieces of thin card with holes punched in the ends; some lengths of ribbon or thin string.

Method

Before the service starts, take the ball of parcel ribbon or string, tie it to a balloon and send it up to the ceiling to measure the length of string you will need so that people can recover their balloons. The string doesn't need to reach to the floor, as long as it can be grabbed. When you have the measurement then cut lots of pieces of string to that length, one for each balloon.

Introduce this prayer activity by announcing that we are going to have a time when we can pray for one another's needs. Invite people to write their prayer needs on a label, reminding them that they will be read by other people. If you have lots of people you can have a label per family group, or you can attach a number to one balloon – although you do need to be using very light card or too many labels may weigh it down. After everyone has written their prayer needs, they take a helium-filled balloon and attach the label and a piece of string or ribbon. Tell people to keep hold of their balloons until the signal is given to let go of them. When everyone is ready, invite people to release their balloons as a symbol of sending their prayers up to God.

Then spend time praying for each other by pulling other people's balloons down on their strings, reading the prayer requests that are written on the labels, praying for them, and sending the prayers back up as you let the balloons go.

Tried & tested

" This prayer method works best if your building doesn't have too high a ceiling! We did this at one of our afternoon services with children attending. They loved the balloons – and some of them took a bit of persuading to let them go! "

13 Lighting a dark world

Resources

You will need: tealights (one per person) in glass holders for safety; photocopies of headings in large type of 'dark' situations in the world – such as suicide, violence, binge drinking, loneliness, people living in fear, unloved children, the forgotten, those in debt, victims of bullying, the grieving, drug addicts, people in pain, current areas of conflict, prisoners of conscience, hostage situations; background music (optional).

Method

Before your service or prayer meeting starts, spread the situations for prayer around different parts of your building or room, so that people can journey from one to another. Agree some sort of signal for when the prayer will end (perhaps when a bell is rung or when the music stops). Begin by having a time when everyone can light their candles together and then dim or turn off your main lights – as long as it's possible to do so without creating hazards or compromising people's health and safety. Remind people that we carry the light of Christ, and that Christ calls us to be lights in a dark world. Then send people out with that light to pray for the dark situations being encountered in different parts of our world. When they come to a piece of paper, invite them to place their light nearby, lighting up the words, and then pray for the people who are suffering.

When they have finished praying for that situation, invite them to pick up their candle, and go to discover another dark area of the world to shine their light on.

Do this activity slowly and thoughtfully. Instrumental music, prayerful songs or plainchant playing in the background while this is going on can be helpful. When the prayer activity is finished, you could place the candles around or on a large cross. Or if you are following the time of prayer with communion, surround the communion table with smaller tables that the lights can be placed on.

Tried & tested

We first did this prayer activity at a special service we had in York Minster on the Feast of the Presentation (sometimes known as Candlemas) when we were thinking about Christ being a 'light to lighten the Gentiles,' as Simeon's prayer puts it in Luke 2. We had the whole of the dark and empty nave of York Minster to play with as there were no chairs in it at the time, and it was amazing seeing the light flicker as people moved around with their candles to pray for the dark corners of the world.

If fire safety is a big problem in your building, you could use glow sticks instead of candles, although the light isn't quite as good.

14 Junk transformed

Resources

You will need: tea lights; plenty of pieces of junk. It's very important to make sure that these items are fireproof, so avoid paper or plastic. You could use crushed drinks cans, empty food tins and lids, broken CD ROMs, empty jars, an old disc drive, a circuit board, a beer bottle. Be sure to warn people about sharp edges and place cans upside down to minimise the possibility of people getting hurt. Check that there is a fire extinguisher or bucket of water close by.

Method

Scatter the junk around the front area of your worship space. It's amazing how quickly the space starts to look like a mini tip! As you do so, talk about people who feel useless and unwanted; those people society has written off, either because they have made mistakes in the past, or because they are broken or disabled in some way. You may like to mention some of the broken people from the Bible, like Peter, Paul or Mary Magdalene. People like this find it difficult to escape their pasts, but God can do amazing things through them.

Invite people to come forward, light a candle and place it on or near one of the pieces of junk and, as they do so, to pray for someone who feels useless, broken or no better than a piece of junk.

As the candles are lit, gradually the junk is illuminated and the bottles and tins begin to shine and reflect the candlelight. Suddenly the pile of junk no longer looks like a tip; it looks like a beautiful collection of candle holders.

Pray that the light of Christ will light up all our lives, especially the lives of those people we have prayed for, to transform us all.

Tried & tested

We did this prayer activity for a chaplains' conference. It's amazingly effective, the way the candlelight transforms the pieces of junk, making them shine with beauty that was not noticeable before. It works best in an evening service or event so that the candlelight contrasts with the darkness.

15 Rags to riches

Resources
You will need: a large cross (one made of two large pieces of old weatherworn wood tied together with old rope works very well); a collection of rags or frayed pieces of material, each long enough to tie around the cross; a small coffee table or step to lean the cross against; background music (optional); the script from page 66.

Method
Read the script slowly, pausing at appropriate points. If you prefer, you could use other Bible verses suitable for introducing a time of confession. After the initial Bible verses, invite people to take a rag from the

collection, which may be passed around or placed on a table in a different part of the room or worship space. Then follow the script, pausing as explained. You may want to play a song of confession, sorrow or a song about the cross while people tie their rags to the cross.

Tried & tested

66 We used a version of this as a creative confession at a church weekend away. The cross looked very beautiful when it was decorated with the rags, but it was also a reminder of the price that Christ had to pay to bring us forgiveness. We sang a version of the Jesus Prayer called 'Have mercy' by COTA (Church of the Apostles) while this was being done. 99

16 Unclean lips

Resources

You will need: a brazier of some kind – we used a wok lid balanced on some bricks; cinder toffee – enough for everyone to have a piece; a red spotlight or a desklamp with a red lighting gel or red 'light cubes'; photocopies of the prayer from page 34.

Cinder toffee

Cinder toffee is an easy home-made sweet made using vinegar and bicarbonate of soda in the mix. These two ingredients react together, frothing before setting into thousands of tiny bubbles and hardening into something like a buttery toffee-flavoured honeycomb of the kind you get inside Cadbury's Crunchie bars.

Ingredients:

        50 g salted butter
        300 ml water
        4 teaspoons malt vinegar
        3 tablespoons golden syrup
        450 g granulated sugar
        1 teaspoon bicarbonate of soda or baking soda

Grease a large baking tin. Heat the butter, water and vinegar together in a very large saucepan (needed because of the frothing!). When the butter has melted, stir in the sugar and syrup until dissolved. Bring to the boil and keep boiling without stirring until a teaspoon of the mixture dropped into a cup of cold water forms into brittle strands that crack when you try to shape them. Remove from the heat and gently stir in the bicarbonate of soda. Frothing occurs! Keep stirring gently until bubbles settle and then pour into the greased tin. After 10-20 minutes the mixture will be set but still warm and you can break it into pieces and lay on a wire rack until cool.

Method

Set up a brazier in a prominent position in your worship space. Fill the brazier with the cinder toffee. Light the brazier with your chosen red light source. Read the story of the call of Isaiah (Isaiah 6:1–8). Then say together the prayer given or an alternative confession prayer.

After the confession you could say a prayer of reassurance of God's forgiveness. Then invite everyone to come up and take a 'coal', touch their lips with it and eat it.

Tried & tested

 We did this prayer activity when the readings one Sunday included the story of the call of Isaiah, when the angel takes a burning coal from the altar and touches Isaiah's lips with it. So we did something similar! At the end of a confession prayer, we invited people to come up to the communion table and take a piece of cinder toffee from an improvised brazier, touch it to their lips and eat it afterwards. It was a very powerful way of telling people that they were forgiven.

17 Create your own desert   Doncaster   29/8/10

Resources
You will need: sandpaper cut into small strips that will roll up into tubes; rubber bands; pens, pencils or felt-tip pens; instrumental background music.

Method
Begin by reading one of the Gospel accounts of Jesus' journey into the desert when he was tempted, such as Luke 4:1–13. Hand out the pieces of sandpaper and pens, one of each per person. Play the music, inviting people to spend about five minutes considering what they could do to spend more time with God.

- How might they be able to create more space to do this?

- Do they need to give something up for a while to allow themselves to do this?

- Is there something extra they could add into their timetable that would help them get closer to God, such as a prayer meeting, a midweek service, a time for Bible reading, or a meditative country walk?

Invite them to jot down their ideas on the back of their piece of sandpaper, reassuring them that no one else will read their writing as it will not be displayed publicly. Pray a prayer that God would speak to each person in the congregation while the music is playing and then allow people time to think, pray and write.

At the end of the time, stop the music and describe how Jesus went into the desert to spend more time with God. The written ideas represent the congregation's own personal deserts.

Give out the rubber bands and invite everyone to roll their piece of sandpaper into a tube, securing it with the rubber band, so that the writing on the inside of the tube can no longer be seen. Then invite them to take the sandpaper tubes home and to place them in a prominent place in the house as a reminder that God wants to spend some personal time with them.

Tried & tested

This prayer activity is particularly meaningful at the beginning of Lent, but could be used at any other time you wished the church to re-evaluate the time they spend with God.

18 Christmas meditation

Resources
You will need: the script from page 67; some Arabic-sounding background music (optional: play very quietly if used).

Method

Simply read the script, slowly and thoughtfully, allowing pauses for people to respond.

19 Floating light

Resources

You will need: a number of glass bowls filled with water; floating candles; matches; pieces of white scrap paper about A6 size; pencils; background music (optional).

Method

Give everyone a piece of paper and a pencil. If you have a small group, also give everyone a candle each. With a larger group, have enough candles to place safely in each glass bowl and volunteers ready to light them.

Explain that you are having a time of intercessory prayer for the world. Invite everyone to think about troubling world situations as you read John 1:1–9 slowly and prayerfully. Ask people to describe some of the situations they have thought about, where people are in darkness, by drawing them on their pieces of paper. Remind people that their level of drawing skill doesn't matter; this activity is about prayer.

You might want to play some music and dim the lights as people are doing this.

When everyone has finished, ask them to place their pieces of paper, drawing side upwards, underneath the glass bowls. Then read Isaiah 9:2–7, while floating candles are carefully lit and placed in the bowls.

When the candles are lit, the light is refracted through the rippling water and it dances beautifully on the drawings. You might see rippling light over armoured tanks or crying children, some of them reflecting onto the walls.

20 Callings trail

Resources

You will need: 15 pieces of paper, each with one section of the **Callings trail** (pages 26–28) printed on them; 15 pieces of blank paper; 15 Bibles; tables, stands or somewhere on the walls to attach writing to; prayerful background music. With larger congregations, multiply the resources two, three or four times to avoid queues.

Method

Place the 15 sections, each representing a different biblical character, in different places around your church or meeting hall, putting a pencil and blank sheet of paper beside each one, and a Bible open at the relevant passages. Explain that you will be exploring the different ways people in the Bible have been called by God. People are free to visit the different stations in any order they wish, to read the scripts and Bible passages, and to add any comments, thoughts or prayers to share with others.

21 Pearls of wisdom

Resources

You will need: pearlised or shiny giftwrap or art paper; pens or pencils; thin knitting needles or darning needles; some strong cotton thread; double-sided tape – ordinary clear tape will work but won't look as tidy.

Method

Cut your wrapping paper into thin triangles, about 3 cm wide at the bottom and tapering to a point. Give one
(Continued on page 29.)

Saul/Paul

Saul sees a blinding flash of light on the road to Damascus and hears the voice of Jesus saying, 'Why do you persecute me?' He is told to go to the city and God sends Ananias to heal his eyesight, talk to him and baptise him. Read Acts 9:1–19. Sometimes we are called by God in dramatic or sudden ways.

The Ethopian official

The Ethiopian official is called through reading the scriptures while he is on a journey. Philip comes alongside his carriage and explains to him the prophecy he is reading, which is about Jesus. It all feels like a bit of a coincidence – but strange coincidences are one of the ways God works. Philip has sensed the voice of God telling him to stay close to the Ethiopian's carriage, setting the scene for the coincidence to happen. Read Acts 8:26–40.

Zacchaeus the tax collector

Jesus doesn't call Zacchaeus to follow him. He just invites himself to stay at Zacchaeus' house for a while. Yet, as a result, Zacchaeus changes his lifestyle and promises to compensate anyone he has cheated in the past. Read Luke 19:1–9.

Sometimes we just need to invite Christ to work in us, and see what happens next.

Matthew, Simon, Andrew, James, John

Jesus simply says, 'Follow me' to Matthew. To Simon and Andrew he says, 'Come with me and I will teach you to fish for people.' With James and John he simply calls them by name. Read Matthew 9:9.

Jeremiah

God tells Jeremiah that he was chosen before he was even born to be a prophet. Jeremiah protests that he is too young to work as a prophet, but God tells him not to object and to go to the people he is sent to. Read Jeremiah 1:4–10. Ask God about his plans for you; he has plans for everyone.

Jonah

Jonah has a 'roundabout' sort of calling. He hears God's voice telling him to go to Nineveh to speak his message to the people there. Jonah goes... in the opposite direction! He boards a ship, gets thrown overboard and ends up in a terrible situation, trapped inside a fish. Finally he promises to do what God wants and goes to Nineveh. Read Jonah 1. Sometimes we are scared of following. What scares you?

Isaiah

Isaiah has an amazing vision of God in the temple and feels very guilty. But an angel comes with a coal from the altar which he touches to his lips in order to purify him. He then hears God appealing for a messenger and volunteers to be the one to go. Read Isaiah 6:1–8. We might not see God in glory in a vision, but maybe we catch glimpses of him. Thank God for the times and places when you have glimpsed God – and the people through whom you have glimpsed him.

Nehemiah

Nehemiah has an emotional calling. He is extremely upset about Jerusalem being in ruins and fasts and prays about it. The king sees he is upset and asks him about it. Nehemiah asks to go to Jerusalem to rebuild it. 'And because the gracious hand of my God was upon me, the king granted my requests.' Read Nehemiah 1. Has God stirred your emotions? Is he stirring them now?

Elisha

Elisha is working hard ploughing a field with his oxen when the prophet Elijah comes to put his cloak on him, calling him to follow him and God. Elisha obviously feels that this is the right thing to do because he 'burns his bridges' by killing his oxen, giving the meat to his relatives and following Elijah. Read 1 Kings 19:19–21. Has someone else ever seen talents or gifts in you? Thank God for those people now. Are there other people within whom you are seeing gifts?

David

God calls David through someone else: Samuel. He sends Samuel to Jesse (David's father) and is told to ignore all the older brothers – who all look better 'king material' – and go for the youngest, David, to anoint as king. God's Spirit fills David at this point, but it is a long time before David actually becomes king. David has to be patient before his calling is fulfilled. Read 1 Samuel 16:1–13. Are there things you are impatient for God to do?

Samuel

Samuel, when still a boy, hears a voice in the middle of the night, which he thinks is the voice of Eli the priest but which is actually God calling him. Read 1 Samuel 3. Have you ever heard the voice of God? In the quietness... in other people... in the Bible? Take some time simply to stop and listen to that voice now.

callingstrail

Gideon

God calls Gideon to rescue the Israelites from their oppressors. An angel appears to him, but he is still not convinced: 'If now I have found favour in your eyes, give me a sign that it is really you talking to me.' The angel sets fire to the food Gideon brings him. Gideon is then terrified and believes that the angel is from God, but still keeps asking for proof from God that he is going to rescue Israel. He puts a fleece on the ground and asks that the dew ends up on the fleece but not on the ground so that he will know that God is going to rescue Israel. Then he asks God to make the ground wet and the fleece dry. God does all this for him. Read Judges 6:11–23. Sometimes God works in miraculous ways. Thank God now for his miraculous power at work in your life.

Moses

God appears to Moses in a burning bush – a really spectacular calling! God wants Moses to go the king of Egypt to help rescue the Israelites from slavery. He gives Moses miraculous powers, such as turning a stick into a snake. Despite this, Moses says, 'No, don't send me. I've never been a good speaker. Please send someone else.' God recruits Aaron to help with the public speaking; and Moses and Aaron go to Pharoah as God has requested. Read Exodus 3:1–14. What things do you feel inadequate about? Ask God to give you courage and confidence about the gifts he has given you.

Jacob

Jacob sees heaven open in a dream and hears God say, 'I will give this land to you and your descendants.' A while later, at a place called Peniel, Jacob wrestles and struggles with God and says, 'I will not let you go until you bless me.' At the end of a night of wrestling, God blesses Jacob and says, 'Your name now will be Israel.' Read Genesis 32:22–30. What do you struggle with? What do you find difficult about following God? Talk to God now about these things.

Abraham

Abraham is originally called to leave his home and go to a new land when he is already 75 years old – which just proves you're never too old to be called by God! When Abraham is 99 years old and childless, God appears to him, drafts a contract and promises that he will be the father of many nations. Later God appears to him at a place called Mamre through three angels. God says that in nine months' time Sarah, Abraham's wife, will have a child. Sarah laughs, then denies having laughed, but nine months later she does have a child, who she names Isaac. Read Genesis 17:1–8,15–19; 18:1,10–15; 21:1–5. Are there promises you have been given that you find hard to imagine taking shape? Is there anything you have been tempted to laugh about in the past that has really happened? Thank God for fulfilled promises, and ask God to increase your faith that miracles can happen and will happen.

of the triangles and a pen or pencil to each member of your group or congregation. Read James 3:15–18 and then the script from page 65, slowly and with appropriate pauses to let people think.

When you have finished the script, invite everyone to take their triangles and wrap them, wide end first, around a darning or knitting needle so that it makes a sort of pearl bead, securing each bead with a small piece of tape. Take the beads off the needles and take them to the front of the church and thread them all onto the cotton to make a garland or necklace of 'pearls'. You could use it to decorate something in your church with it. If it's Christmas time, you could use it as a tree decoration. If it's a communion service, you could lay it on the communion table or around the cross.

22 White stones

Resources
You will need: some white stones – which can be bought in packets from garden centres; a large bowl; some permanent OHP pens; the script from page 69; some gentle background music (optional).

Method
At the front of the worship space, set up a large bowl, preferably glass, with white stones in it. Read the script slowly, pausing where it's helpful.

23 Stone meditation

Resources
You will need: a pile of stones or rocks – beach cobbles sold in garden centres work very well; the script from page 70.

Method
Read the script. At the end of the meditation you may wish to give people the choice of a couple of different places where they can offer their stones. If you are using this meditation during a communion service, you could invite people to place their stones around the table or altar. Other options would be to have a cairn where people can pile their stones, a cross they can deposit their stones beneath, or a pool that they can place their stones around or within.

24 Decorating the cloth

Resources
You will need: an attractive piece of cloth, large enough to go over your communion table. I suggest you buy something specially, just in case it gets marked! We have a lovely piece of voile with gold embroidery that we bought in a sale. Also: washable felt-tip pens; kneelers or cushions (optional); background worship music (optional).

Method
Place the cloth and the felt-tip pens where people can easily access them. If you are working with younger people, you could put them on the floor surrounded by kneelers or cushions. Older people may prefer to work at a table. It's better, though, to use a different table from the communion table, because there's something very meaningful about moving the cloth to drape it over the communion table after the prayers and before putting the bread and wine on it.

If you have a very large congregation it may be better to have three or four cloths. If you use net, muslin or voile, the prayers will be visible as the layers are built up on the table. However, if you use net or voile, make sure you have a base cloth or paper underneath or you may get felt-tip marks on whatever you were leaning on and your church cleaner will not be happy with you!

When you have arranged your cloths and pens, invite people to write their own prayers of intercession for people or situations that are on their hearts at the time. As this activity can last some time, play some appropriate music while people are quietly working and praying.

After the cloths have been draped on the communion table, add the bread and wine and celebrate communion together. At the end of the service, allow some time for people to read the prayers that others have written. If you soak the cloths afterwards, you may be able to

[handwritten note: Write something that you would not like to see change. These go into a barrier (Bricks). Write something that you would be willing to forgo. These could go into a cog.]

25 Praying for the excluded

This prayer activity could be used during a service focusing on a number of different Bible passages: the cleansing of the ten people suffering with leprosy (Luke 17:11–19); the good Samaritan (Luke 10:30–37); the woman who had been bleeding for 12 years (Mark 5:21–34); or the Canaanite woman (Matthew 15:22–28).

Resources

You will need: a portable fence of some kind. We used puppy fencing which comes in four pieces with hinges at each corner. Also: a communion table or some other symbol of God's presence, such as a cross; strips of coloured paper large enough to write on and be seen, that can be woven through or stick onto the bars of your fence; a marker pen; a 'No entry' sign.

Method

On pieces of one particular colour, write labels giving categories of the kinds of people who weren't allowed to pray in the inner courts of the temple and attach to the fence. You can get lots of inspiration for these labels from the books of Leviticus and Deuteronomy. Your list will include categories like women, pork-eaters, people with eczema, people with leprosy, Gentiles, etc.

If you are having a communion service later, use your fence to fence off the table with the bread and wine on it. Add your 'No entry' sign.

Then proceed with your service or meeting as normal. When the time comes for the prayers, invite people to take pieces of paper of a different colour and write on them the names of groups of people who are excluded from our society today, and weave them through or stick them to the fence. Your groups will include categories like drug addicts, the severely disabled, people with mental health problems, ex-offenders and so on.

Then, when the time comes to celebrate communion, read this passage from Hebrews 10:19–24, using the TNIV translation:

> Therefore, brothers and sisters, since we have confidence to enter the Most Holy Place by the blood of Jesus, by a new and living way opened for us through the curtain, that is, his body, and since we have a great priest over the house of God, let us draw near to God with a sincere heart in full assurance of faith, having our hearts sprinkled to cleanse us from a guilty conscience and having our bodies washed with pure water. Let us hold unswervingly to the hope we profess, for he who promised is faithful. And let us consider how we may spur one another on toward love and good deeds.

Then open the fence and turn it the other way round, so that the people groups who were previously kept outside are now in the inner place, around the table. This time, leave a gap so the fence becomes a sort of backdrop to the table and continue with your communion service. If you are not planning to celebrate communion, you will still need to open the fence and place it the other way round, but you might want to invite people to come into the space and do some other activity such as touching a cross in a gesture of thanksgiving or lighting candles around a cross as an act of celebration.

26 Living stones

Resources

You will need: a long piece of blue fabric to represent a river; rocks or cobbles (available from garden centres); the script on page 69.

Method

Arrange your river in meandering fashion around your prayer and worship space. Give out a rock to each member of the congregation or prayer group. Invite everyone to get into a comfortable position. Read Revelation 21, or extracts from it; then read the script slowly, pausing where appropriate.

27 Balloons 2

Resources

You will need: balloons; felt-tip pens – with points that are not too sharp!

Method

Invite people to write their prayer needs on a deflated balloon using a felt-tip pen. They can then swap the balloon if they wish and inflate someone else's balloon, praying over their needs as they do so. Alternatively people can inflate their own balloon and pray over their own needs and the needs of others in a small group of three or four. Tell them not to knot the necks.

At the end of the time of prayer, give a signal which invites everyone to let go of their balloons at the same time, and watch them whoosh upwards and around the building as a symbol of our prayers going up to God.

Finally, invite everyone to collect up a balloon, take it home, and pray during the week for the person who wrote those prayer needs on that balloon.

28 White noise

Resources

You will need: an old television – or several if you have a larger group; a power extension to plug in your television; non-permanent whiteboard markers; cloths for wiping the screens.

Method

Switch on the television and adjust the brightness so when you start writing on the screen it can be seen. The TV should be showing 'snow'. Point out that the reason the television is showing snow is because it is not receiving a signal from an aerial. It is having problems communicating.

Ask your group or congregation to think about people who are having problems communicating with one another on an international level – world leaders in situations of conflict. Invite people to come up and write a name or situation on the television screen.

Then pray silently or out loud for those situations. At the end of the prayers, write 'Amen' on the television and rub off the writing with a cloth.

Then invite people to think about a situation where people are having problems communicating with each other on a local level – perhaps within families or local government or any other situations that are in the news at the moment. Once again, ask people to come up and list those situations on the screen.

As before, pray, write 'Amen' and clean off the screen.

Next, invite your group to think about people who find it hard to communicate with God – perhaps because they find it difficult to believe, or because they blame God for something that has happened. Follow the same process of writing, praying and wiping off.

29 Mint

Resources

You will need: fresh mint leaves; a Thermos flask or kettle filled with boiling water; some metal or pottery jugs, teacups or small paper espresso cups; the script on page 68. Although it might be tempting to use a teapot, the mint flavour will be tainted by the ordinary tea, unless it's a brand new teapot.

Method

Give a mint leaf to each member of the group or congregation, invite them to sit in a relaxed position and quieten themselves, and then read out the script slowly and prayerfully.

Invite everyone to put their leaves into the jug and then read Revelation 22:1,2:

> Then the angel showed me the river of the water of life, as clear as crystal, flowing from the throne of God and of the Lamb down the middle of the great street of the city. On each side of the river stood the tree of life, bearing twelve crops of fruit, yielding its fruit every month. And the leaves of the tree are for the healing of the nations.

While you are reading this, pour boiling water onto the mint leaves. Invite people to come up and get their cup of tea or delegate volunteers with trays to pass the tea around. As people drink their tea, invite them to think about what they would like healing for. Encourage them to name those things before God in prayer.

Tried & tested

 One of the wonderful things about this prayer activity is that the smell of the mint tea fills the room as the water is poured on the crushed leaves.

30 Scars

Resources

You will need: some small plant pots, preferably one per person; pea seeds; soil; scoops or large spoons;

small pieces of paper; pencils or pens; small plastic bags to place the completed pots inside; photocopies of the poem on page 34 or an OHP displaying the words of the poem (optional).

Method

Begin by reading the poem together. Then invite everyone to take a piece of paper and a pencil and write their scars and hurts as a prayer. Tell people that no one else will read this prayer and so they are free to be as personal as they wish. Then ask everyone to fold their piece of paper so that the writing cannot be seen and place it at the bottom of a small plant pot, putting soil on top of it, and then planting a pea seed.

Encourage everyone to take their pot home in a plastic bag, assuring them that hope can grow even in very dark, sad and scarred places. As they water their pea seed every day, they should pray for the other people who did this activity, for healing for their scars and hurts.

Peas grow quite quickly, so hopefully there will be little green shoots of hope and new life popping up soon in the pots! You could invite people to return their peas at a later date so people can see the growth and hopefully testify to feeling healed.

Tried & tested

 We did this prayer activity when the Gospel reading for the day was about Thomas (John 20:24–29). We thought about his doubts and how Christ appeared to him and showed him his scars, and this led us into prayer. The beautiful thing about this prayer activity is that people can pray together about some very deep concerns, while they remain private.

31 God's vineyard

Resources

You will need: the script on page 71.

Method

Ask people to get themselves comfortable and relaxed, to close their eyes and, as they become aware of any worries that come into their minds, to gently hand each one over to God. Read the Parable of the Tenants (Matthew 21:33–46) and then the script, slowly and prayerfully, pausing wherever it seems appropriate.

32 Christ the King

Resources

You will need: a crown of thorns – make one using twigs from a thorn bush (berberis works well) and wire; a red cushion; leaf shapes made from green paper (fold the paper when cutting to make several at once); pens, pencils or felt-tip pens; desk lamp (optional); background music (optional).

Method

Before your service or prayer event begins, place the crown of thorns on the red cushion in a prominent place in your worship space. You may want to illuminate it using a desk lamp or spotlight.

When people have gathered and it is time to pray, invite people to take some green leaves and to write on each a one-sentence prayer for situations they would like Christ to rule over and change. While the prayers are being written you could play some music or sing a song on the theme of Christ being the ruler of all.

When everyone has finished, invite them to (carefully!) place a leaf onto one of the thorns. When all the leaves have been placed on the crown of thorns, point out the similarity to a laurel wreath of triumph and remind everyone that Christ will triumph over all these problems.

Show me your scars

Show me your scars;
I have shown you mine;
I have let you touch them;
Tell me where it still hurts.

The scar from long ago
Or the more recent wound;
Let me see your hands;
Let me see inside your side.

Show me your scars;
Into your heartbreak,
Into your memories,
Let me heal your pain.

Prayer: Unclean lips

We confess, that we too are a people of unclean lips,
And we live among a people of unclean lips
Who use words as weapons to crush the weak,
To bully, blaspheme and stab others in the back.

Yet we long to see the King, the Lord of Hosts.
Forgive us when we fail to hear your call,
Fail to listen to your voice,
Fail to speak your words.
Forgive us and make us clean.

33 Prayer meal

Resources

You will need: food and drinks organised into different courses, using the list below as a guide but adapting to suit your own needs; plates, glasses, cutlery etc; candles and matches; table decorations (optional).

Method

The idea is to sit around a table sharing a meal, praying between courses and linking the prayer themes to the food. During the courses, people have opportunity to eat and talk normally after the prayer times, especially during the main course which takes longer to eat.

1st course: fasting

With empty plates in front of you, light candles and pray for the hungry, for those who are ill, and for those fasting to be close to God today.

2nd course: starter and drinks

Give everyone a choice of two starters, such as poppadoms or breadsticks; and a choice of two drinks, such as red wine or white wine, cola or orange juice. When everyone is served, pray for countries having to make choices through elections; or for anyone you know faced with difficult decisions.

3rd course: main dish

Serve a casserole or something similar and side dishes of vegetables. Pray for your group or church with all its various gifts and struggles. And then pray for environmental issues.

4th course: dessert

Serve cherry crumble made with unstoned cherries. Place empty bowls in the middle of the table and each time anyone finds a stone in the crumble they place it in a bowl and, as they do so, name a person they know who needs prayer and, if relevant, they can name a specific situation.

A variation on this is to serve nuts for dessert and to place the shells in bowls as the prompt for prayer – but be very careful to check that no one in your group is allergic to nuts. Or you could serve fruit that needs peeling such as clementines, placing the peel in the bowls.

Tried & tested

This idea first came as a result of a conversation we were having about a prayer meeting which involved food. We were trying to decide whether to pray before or after we ate and suddenly had the idea of actually interleaving the prayer with the food.

The part of the prayer meal that everyone appreciated the most was the part involving cherry stones.

There were no set subjects for discussion between the prayer times, but we found that discussion naturally gravitated to the prayer topics.

34 Hands meditation

Resources

You will need: the script on page 72; some olive oil.

Method

Read the account of Thomas meeting the risen Jesus in John 20:19–30. Invite your congregation or prayer group to get comfortable. Before you start reading the script, explain that for this meditation it would be good to sit within easy reach of another person. At some point in the meditation people will be encouraged to hold someone else's hand. If anyone is uncomfortable with this for any reason, they should feel free to move into a space further away now and simply imagine holding someone's hand.

Read the script slowly and thoughtfully. Afterwards, invite everyone to ask their neighbour if they would like their hands blessed with oil. Circulate the olive oil. As each person marks their neighbour's palms with a small cross in oil with their fingers, they can pray this prayer: 'May Christ bless your hands. May they be healing hands which he can use to touch a hurting world.'

35 The hem of his garment

Resources
You will need: a long coat – this could be a modern long winter coat or the sort of coat that Jesus might have worn; a coat hanger; string; something to hang the string from, such as a beam or hook in the wall; small pieces of scrap material; felt-tip pens; safety pins; a portable CD player and the track 'Hem of his garment' by Faithless and Dido (optional).

Method
Before the service or meeting starts, place the coat on a coat hanger, and place it where it can be seen by everyone. If possible, it's best to suspend the whole hanger from a beam in the ceiling, so that it hangs in the centre of the worship space, but low enough so that people can touch the coat and pin fabric to it.

Read the story of the woman with the issue of blood from Mark 5:25–34. Hand out little pieces of scrap fabric and pens. Ask everyone to think of someone they know who has been ill or in pain for a long time. They can spend a few minutes praying for those people silently, and then write their first name or initials on their piece of fabric.

Then encourage your group to come up and pin these prayers onto the coat. While this is happening, you may wish to play the track 'Hem of his garment' which includes the lines:

Oh I wish I could be
touched by the hem of his garment.

When the service has finished you might want to invite people to take home a piece of fabric and pray for the person whose name or initials are written on it during the following week.

36 Alphabet prayers

(with thanks to Paul Millard)

Resources
You will need: cards with letters of the alphabet on them – Lexicon or Scrabble tiles work well.

Method
Shuffle the cards or tiles and pick one at random, praying for every situation that springs to mind beginning with that letter. For example, if you get the letter A, you could pray for Afghanistan, alcoholics and so on. Pick a different letter and pray again.

In a larger meeting or service, you could hand the cards or tiles out around the congregation, inviting each person to pray silently for situations that come to mind beginning with the letter they have received. When the prayer time has finished you can invite people to take their letters and place them around the communion table or at the foot of the cross as a way of giving those situations into God's hands.

“ We did this prayer activity at a church staff prayer meeting. Afterwards people commented that the restriction of using letters enabled them to pray for situations that they would not have thought about otherwise. ”

37 Praying with Rublev

Doncaster 5/9/10

Some people are suspicious of icons, citing the prohibition on making images in the Ten Commandments, yet icons have become increasingly popular as aids to prayer in recent years, probably due to the popularity of the Taizé community in France. Many people are unaware that the Orthodox Church, which produces many icons, actually forbids the carving of religious images or the portrayal of the Father – precisely because of the prohibition in the Ten Commandments. Icon painters are only allowed to portray what has already been revealed. They cannot portray the Father but they can portray Jesus because, 'No one has ever seen God. The only Son ... has shown us what God is like' (John 1:18 CEV). Many icons are actually symbolic rather than realistic (again to discourage idolatry) and they almost have the quality of visual sermons.

One of the most famous icons is a painting by Andrei Rublev dating from around 1410. It is often known as the 'Old Testament Trinity' yet, strictly speaking, it is portraying the story of the hospitality of Abraham, when he entertains three angels (Genesis 18). This prayer activity uses that picture as an inspiration and aid to prayer.

Resources

You will need: the script from page 73; a projection or copy of the Rublev icon that can be clearly seen by everyone; paper printouts of the icon for people to take home afterwards (optional). There are many copies of this image available on the web as it is out of copyright.

Method

Begin by introducing people to the Rublev icon scene. Do this by reading Genesis 18:1–10a. Then read section A of the script while people are looking at the icon image. Then invite people to relax into an attitude of prayer as you read section B slowly, pausing where needed.

38 Local icons

Resources

You will need: a collection of extracts and pictures from local newspapers, magazines and leaflets, sorted into different colours; images from the life of your church community (optional); a large piece of paper, card or fabric; glue or double-sided tape; fat marker pens; a data projector or OHP; a large image of an icon (such as Rublev's Trinity) or picture of Jesus, a cross, a trinity knot or another simple religious symbol to copy.

Method

Pin or tape your icon image on the wall and point a projector at it. Then trace the outline of the image in pencil. When you are happy with it, go over your lines in marker pen. Colour code different parts of the image and write the names of your colours on those areas in pencil.

When you are ready to pray, place the 'icon' on the ground. Invite people to pick up some of the magazine and newspaper extracts and to pray for the situations that come to mind when they see those images. You could talk through some examples. When they have prayed, encourage them to stick those images onto the area of the 'icon' of the correct colour. Continue until the icon is completely covered, or until the prayer time is finished.

Hang the 'icon' in the worship space so that everyone can see the results. You may wish to leave it with a notice inviting people who see the picture to pray for their local community.

39 Road to Emmaus

Resources
You will need: photocopies of the 32 panels on pages 39–47, which lay out some of the messianic prophecies about Jesus and their New Testament fulfilments. You could print the 'prophecy' and 'prophecy fulfilled' passages on different coloured pieces of paper so that people can easily spot which is which. You also need: a bell or some other sort of signal to invite people to return; a third piece of paper near each pair of papers so that people can write their own prayers of thanksgiving or praise (optional); pens or pencils (optional).

Method
Before your service or meeting begins, lay out the prayer trail or road around your worship space. Then, when you are ready to begin your time of prayer, read the story of the Emmaus road from Luke 24:13–27. Explain that although we can't have quite the same experience as the disciples did, we too can have our hearts burn with wonder, by taking a journey along the Emmaus road and reading the prophecies about Jesus. Also, remind them that Jesus will walk the road with them too, for he promised that where two or three are gathered in his name, he would be there also (Matthew 18:20). Begin the journey with a prayer and then invite people to begin their own Emmaus journey through the prophecies about Jesus in their own time. Read Luke 24:25–27 again as people set off.

Tried & tested

We did this prayer activity in York Minster by night. It was amazing having a building that large in which to do our journey to Emmaus, as it felt like we were travelling quite a way. But you can still do this in a smaller building. Use other rooms besides your main worship space if they are available.

40 Heaven's door

Resources
You will need: no special equipment apart from a Bible and the script from pages 75 and 76.

Method
Begin by reading Revelation 4:1–8, and then read the script, slowly and meditatively.

41 Grief transformed

Resources
You will need: a safe place to have a bonfire – preferably outside; some small sticks of kindling – often sold in petrol stations – enough for one each; biro pens; a large tall candle – sold for Easter in some Christian shops; lots of smaller candles – the ones sold with cardboard rings around them to prevent wax dripping onto your hand are ideal; the script from page 71; background music (optional).

Method
Start your fire 15 to 30 minutes before the service to allow it time to get going. Then, inside your building, give out the pieces of kindling and biros, reassuring people that no one is going to read what they are going to write on them. (Continued on page 48.)

prophecies

1 PROPHECY – the serpent will strike the heel of the woman's offspring.
Genesis 3:15:

> And I will put enmity
>> between you and the woman,
>> and between your offspring and hers;
> he will crush your head,
>> and you will strike his heel.

2 PROPHECY FULFILLED – the 'heel' is often interpreted as being the whole foot and reminds us of Christ's feet being pierced on the cross. Interestingly, fresh light on this may have been given to us when, in 1968, archaeologists discovered the body of a crucified man north of Jerusalem. This man died around AD 7 and so was quite a close contemporary of Jesus, suggesting that the two crucifixions may well have been carried out in a similar way. The body had a heel bone with a curved nail stuck through it – apparently the nail was driven through the heel bones from the side rather than through the feet. Perhaps this means that the prophecy was fulfilled more literally than we previously thought.

3 PROPHECY – the book of Exodus tells of the Passover in which the blood from the sacrifice of a lamb saved the people from the angel of death. The people crossed over from slavery to the promised land at the end of their journey. Exodus 12:1–13:

> The LORD said to Moses and Aaron in Egypt, "This month is to be for you the first month, the first month of your year. Tell the whole community of Israel that on the tenth day of this month each man is to take a lamb for his family, one for each household. If any household is too small for a whole lamb, they must share one with their nearest neighbour, having taken into account the number of people there are. You are to determine the amount of lamb needed in accordance with what each person will eat. The animals you choose must be year-old males without defect, and you may take them from the sheep or the goats. Take care of them until the fourteenth day of the month, when all the people of the community of Israel must slaughter them at twilight. Then they are to take some of the blood and put it on the sides and tops of the doorframes of the houses where they eat the lambs. That same night they are to eat the meat roasted over the fire, along with bitter herbs, and bread made without yeast. Do not eat the meat raw or cooked in water, but roast it over the fire – head, legs and inner parts. Do not leave any of it till morning; if some is left till morning, you must burn it. This is how you are to eat it: with your cloak tucked into your belt, your sandals on your feet and your staff in your hand. Eat it in haste; it is the LORD's Passover.
>
> On that same night I will pass through Egypt and strike down every firstborn – both men and animals – and I will bring judgement on all the gods of Egypt. I am the LORD. The blood will be a sign for you on the houses where you are; and when I see the blood, I will pass over you. No destructive plague will touch you when I strike Egypt."

4 PROPHECY FULFILLED – the whole Exodus journey can be interpreted as prophecy in action; the Passover from slavery to freedom prefigures our 'passover' from the slavery of wrongdoing, pain and death to the promised land of heaven.

prophecies

5 PROPHECY – one of the regulations for the Passover lamb was that the bones should not be broken. Exodus 12:46:

> It must be eaten inside one house; take none of the meat outside the house. Do not break any of the bones.

6 PROPHECY FULFILLED – Christ's bones were not broken by the soldiers. John 19:33,34:

> But when they came to Jesus and found that he was already dead, they did not break his legs. Instead, one of the soldiers pierced Jesus' side with a spear, bringing a sudden flow of blood and water.

7 PROPHECY – on their way through the desert to the Promised Land, the Israelites were bitten by poisonous snakes. Moses commanded them to lift up a bronze snake on a pole in the desert. Whoever looked at the snake would live. Numbers 21:8:

> The LORD said to Moses, "Make a snake and put it up on a pole; anyone who is bitten can look at it and live."

8 PROPHECY FULFILLED – the lifting up of Jesus on the cross was to heal and save us. John 3:14,16:

> Just as Moses lifted up the snake in the desert, so the Son of Man must be lifted up ...

> For God so loved the world that he gave his one and only Son, that whoever believes in him shall not perish but have eternal life.

9 PROPHECY – a close friend will betray Jesus. Psalm 41:9; Psalm 55:12,13:

> Even my close friend, whom I trusted,
> > he who shared my bread,
> > has lifted up his heel against me.
>
> If an enemy were insulting me,
> > I could endure it;
> if a foe were raising himself against me,
> > I could hide from him.
> But it is you, a man like myself,
> > my companion, my close friend...

10 PROPHECY FULFILLED – Jesus was betrayed by Judas, one of his disciples. Mark 14:18,19:

> While they were reclining at the table eating, he said, "I tell you the truth, one of you will betray me – one who is eating with me.
>
> They were saddened, and one by one they said to him, 'Surely not I?"

11 PROPHECY – the prophets declared that the Messiah or Anointed One had to die and spoke of the manner of his death. Zechariah 12:10; Isaiah 53:2-7:

> And I will pour out on the house of David and the inhabitants of Jerusalem a spirit of grace and supplication. They will look on me, the one they have pierced, and they will mourn for him as one mourns for an only child, and grieve bitterly for him as one grieves for a firstborn son.
>
> He grew up before him like a tender shoot,
>   and like a root out of dry ground.
>   He had no beauty or majesty to attract us to him,
>   nothing in his appearance that we should desire him.
>
> He was despised and rejected by men,
>   a man of sorrows, and familiar with suffering.
>   Like one from whom men hide their faces
>   he was despised, and we esteemed him not.
>
> Surely he took up our infirmities
>   and carried our sorrows,
>   yet we considered him stricken by God,
>   smitten by him, and afflicted.
>
> But he was pierced for our transgressions,
>   he was crushed for our iniquities;
>   the punishment that brought us peace was upon him,
>   and by his wounds we are healed.
>
> We all, like sheep, have gone astray,
>   each of us has turned to his own way;
>   and the Lord has laid on him
>   the iniquity of us all.
>
> He was oppressed and afflicted,
>   yet he did not open his mouth;
>   he was led like a lamb to the slaughter,
>   and as a sheep before her shearers is silent,
>   so he did not open his mouth.

12 PROPHECY FULFILLED – like a sheep before the shearers, Jesus is silent when questioned by Herod. Luke 23:8,9:

> When Herod saw Jesus, he was greatly pleased, because for a long time he had been wanting to see him. From what he had heard about him, he hoped to see him perform some miracle. He plied him with many questions, but Jesus gave him no answer.

prophecies

13 **PROPHECY** – Christ will be mocked, have his hands and feet pierced and feel forsaken by God. Psalm 22:1,6–8,15–18:

My God, my God, why have you forsaken me?
Why are you so far from saving me,
so far from the words of my groaning?

But I am a worm and not a man,
scorned by men and despised by the people.

All who see me mock me;
they hurl insults, shaking their heads:

"He trusts in the LORD;
let the LORD rescue him.
Let him deliver him,
since he delights in him."

My strength is dried up like a potsherd,
and my tongue sticks to the roof of my mouth;
you lay me in the dust of death.

Dogs have surrounded me;
a band of evil men has encircled me,
they have pierced my hands and my feet.

I can count all my bones;
people stare and gloat over me.

They divide my garments among them
and cast lots for my clothing.

14 **PROPHECY FULFILLED** – Christ was ridiculed, and felt alienated from his Father. Matthew 27:41–46:

In the same way the chief priests, the teachers of the law and the elders mocked him. "He saved others" they said, "but he can't save himself! He's the king of Israel! Let him come down now from the cross, and we will believe in him. He trusts in God. Let God rescue him now if he wants him, for he said, 'I am the Son of God'." In the same way the robbers who were crucified with him also heaped insults on him.

From the sixth hour until the ninth hour darkness came over all the land. About the ninth hour Jesus cried out in a loud voice, "Eloi, Eloi, lama sabachthani?" – which means, "My God, my God, why have you forsaken me?"

15 PROPHECY – Christ will be mocked, spat on and beaten. Isaiah 50:6,7:

I offered my back to those who beat me,
    my cheeks to those who pulled out my beard;
    I did not hide my face
    from mocking and spitting.

Because the Sovereign LORD helps me,
    I will not be disgraced.
    Therefore have I set my face like flint,
    and I know I will not be put to shame.

16 PROPHECY FULFILLED – Jesus was treated in just this way. Luke 22:63; Matthew 26:67:

The men who were guarding Jesus began mocking and beating him.

Then they spit in his face and struck him with their fists. Others slapped him...

17 PROPHECY – Christ will be offered gall and vinegar. Psalm 69:21:

They put gall in my food
    and gave me vinegar for my thirst.

18 PROPHECY FULFILLED – Christ was offered gall and vinegar. Matthew 27:33,34; John 19:28,29:

They came to a place called Golgotha (which means The Place of the Skull). There they offered Jesus wine to drink, mixed with gall; but after tasting it, he refused to drink it.

Later, knowing that all was now completed, and so that the Scripture would be fulfilled, Jesus said, 'I am thirsty.' A jar of wine vinegar was there, so they soaked a sponge in it, put the sponge on a stalk of the hyssop plant, and lifted it to Jesus' lips.

19 PROPHECY – there will be an earthquake at the crucifixion and the sun will go down at noon. Amos 8:8,9:

Will not the land tremble for this,
    and all who live in it mourn?
    The whole land will rise like the Nile;
    it will be stirred up and then sink
    like the river of Egypt.

"In that day," declares the Sovereign LORD,
"I will make the sun go down at noon
and darken the earth in broad daylight."

prophecies

20 PROPHECY FULFILLED – there was darkness and shaking of the earth.
Matthew 27:45,51:

> From the sixth hour until the ninth hour darkness came over all the land ... At that moment the curtain of the temple was torn in two from top to bottom. The earth shook and the rocks split.

21 PROPHECY – the prophet Isaiah says that Jesus will die because we did wrong, and that Jesus will die with the wicked and will lie in a tomb of a rich man.
Isaiah 53:8,9:

> By oppression and judgment he was taken away.
>   And who can speak of his descendants?
>   For he was cut off from the land of the living;
>   for the transgression of my people he was stricken.
>
> He was assigned a grave with the wicked,
>   and with the rich in his death,
>   though he had done no violence,
>   nor was any deceit in his mouth.

22 PROPHECY FULFILLED – Joseph of Arimathea provided a burial place.
Matthew 27:57–60:

> As evening approached, there came a rich man from Arimathea, named Joseph, who had himself become a disciple of Jesus. Going to Pilate, he asked for Jesus' body, and Pilate ordered that it be given to him. Joseph took the body, wrapped it in a clean linen cloth, and placed it in his own new tomb that he had cut out of the rock. He rolled a big stone in front of the entrance to the tomb and went away.

23 PROPHECY – Christ will be brought up from the grave. Psalm 30:2,3:

> O LORD my God, I called to you for help
>   and you healed me.
>
> O LORD, you brought me up from the grave;
>   you spared me from going down into the pit.

24 PROPHECY FULFILLED – Jesus was brought up from the grave at the resurrection and his body spared from decay. Mark 16:1–8:

When the Sabbath was over, Mary Magdalene, Mary the mother of James, and Salome bought spices so that they might go to anoint Jesus' body. Very early on the first day of the week, just after sunrise, they were on their way to the tomb and they asked each other, "Who will roll the stone away from the entrance of the tomb?"

But when they looked up, they saw that the stone, which was very large, had been rolled away. As they entered the tomb, they saw a young man dressed in a white robe sitting on the right side, and they were alarmed.

"Don't be alarmed," he said. "You are looking for Jesus the Nazarene, who was crucified. He has risen! He is not here. See the place where they laid him. But go, tell his disciples and Peter, 'He is going ahead of you into Galilee. There you will see him, just as he told you'."

Trembling and bewildered, the women went out and fled from the tomb. They said nothing to anyone, because they were afraid.

25 PROPHECY – there were many prophecies that Jesus was going to rise from the dead, including those from the prophet Hosea and David the psalmist. Hosea 6:1; Psalm 16:9,10:

"Come, let us return to the LORD.
    He has torn us to pieces
    but he will heal us;
    he has injured us
    but he will bind up our wounds."

Therefore my heart is glad and my tongue rejoices;
    my body also will rest secure
because you will not abandon me to the grave,
    nor will you let your Holy One see decay.

26 PROPHECY FULFILLED – on the third day, Jesus rose from the dead. Luke 24:5:

In their fright the women bowed down with their faces to the ground, but the men said to them, "Why do you look for the living among the dead?"

prophecies

27 PROPHECY – Christ will suffer as a guilt offering and bear the sins of many, but after his suffering he will see life. Isaiah 53:10–12:

Yet it was the LORD's will to crush him and cause him to suffer,
and though the LORD makes his life a guilt offering,
he will see his offspring and prolong his days,
and the will of the LORD will prosper in his hand.

After the suffering of his soul,
he will see the light of life and be satisfied;
by his knowledge my righteous servant will justify many,
and he will bear their iniquities.

Therefore I will give him a portion among the great,
and he will divide the spoils with the strong,
because he poured out his life unto death,
and was numbered with the transgressors.
For he bore the sin of many,
and made intercession for the transgressors.

28 PROPHECY FULFILLED – Jesus took the punishment for our sins. 1 John 2:2:

He is the atoning sacrifice for our sins, and not only for ours but also for the sins of the whole world.

29 PROPHECY – the price of betrayal would be thirty pieces of silver, which would be used to buy a potter's field. Zechariah 11:12,13:

I told them, "If you think it best, give me my pay; but if not, keep it." So they paid me thirty pieces of silver.

And the LORD said to me, "Throw it to the potter" – the handsome price at which they priced me! So I took the thirty pieces of silver and threw them into the house of the LORD to the potter.

30 PROPHECY FULFILLED – Judas' fee is returned to the temple, and the potter's field is bought with it. Matthew 27:3–7:

When Judas, who had betrayed him, saw that Jesus was condemned, he was seized with remorse and returned the thirty silver coins to the chief priests and the elders. "I have sinned," he said, "for I have betrayed innocent blood."

"What is that to us?" they replied. "That's your responsibility."

So Judas threw the money into the temple and left. Then he went away and hanged himself.

The chief priests picked up the coins and said, "It is against the law to put this into the treasury, since it is blood money." So they decided to use the money to buy the potter's field as a burial place for foreigners.

31 PROPHECY – in Genesis we read of Abraham's willingness to sacrifice his only son Isaac – a picture of Christ. Genesis 22:7b,8:

> "The fire and wood are here," Isaac said, "but where is the lamb for the burnt offering?" Abraham answered, "God himself will provide the lamb for the burnt offering, my son." And the two of them went on together.

God did provide the lamb; Isaac didn't have to die. Abraham put a distressed ram caught in thorns out of its misery by sacrificing it instead. But ultimately Christ was the lamb that was provided.

32 PROPHECY FULFILLED – John the Baptist recognised the coming sacrifice of Jesus. John 1:29:

> The next day John saw Jesus coming toward him and said, "Look, the Lamb of God, who takes away the sin of the world!"

Set the scene: the apostles were grieving and heartbroken on Holy Saturday. They had lost everything that was dear to them. Invite people to write on their sticks any personal grief, hurts or losses they are experiencing. Play some music while this is happening, and allow people enough time to reflect and write.

When everyone is ready, invite them outside to toss their kindling on the fire. When everyone's sticks have gone into the fire, read the script. After the script, light the big candle and take it inside, with everyone following. Then invite everyone to light their small candles from the large one or from each other's candles. You could then sing an Easter song.

Tried & tested

We did this prayer activity at a vigil service on the evening before Easter Sunday. It was immensely powerful watching our griefs transformed in the new light of the resurrection of Christ.

If you are able to keep the light levels fairly dim in the building during this activity, it prevents people looking over at other people's pieces of wood and makes everyone feel safer about what they are writing.

42 Church prayer trail

If you have an historic building, you could write a prayer trail that can be used not just by your congregation or prayer group, but also by visitors to your building. If you don't have your own building, you could still create a prayer trail around the hall or school where you meet – but the symbols would probably be quite different.

Resources
You will need: your prayer trail written out, perhaps several copies. Laminating them will make them last longer.

Method
Write out a form of words for people to use meditatively as they walk slowly around your building, making comments about any relevant features. The following guidelines will help you decide what to include and the kinds of things to write about them.

Prayer trail guidelines

Take a good look around this building. Do any items particularly strike you?

If you have a font or baptistry...
Place this so that people can see it, and perhaps fill it with water. Invite people to write a prayer of thanks for the gift of water and to pray for those who have no access to clean water. Those who have been baptised can thank God for their baptism, for the fact that when we are sorry we can have a new start, and for being able to be part of the community of the church.

If you have pictures in the windows, or sculptures...
Are there pictures in the windows? Who do these pictures represent? If they are pictures of saints, what is their story? Are there aspects of their story that lead you to prayer for someone in a similar situation – for example, a representation of a martyr might lead you to prayer for those who are in prison at the moment because of their faith in Jesus; or a preacher might lead you into prayer for evangelists and missionaries today.

If you have musical instruments...
Is there a piano or organ, guitar or stereo? If there is, you could write a prayer of thanks for the gift of music.

Invite people to think about their favourite pieces of music or those that have been played at important moments in their lives, such as at family weddings, and to thank God for those moments.

If you have an altar or communion table...

What does it look like? Does it have an altar cloth or covering? What is pictured on that covering? For example, if there are pictures of wheat or grapes you could pray for farmers, and for those who work in food production. If your building uses different coloured seasonal coverings such as purple during Advent, red at Pentecost or white and gold at times of celebration, you may want to pray as a response to those colours and what they suggest to you. For example, purple is a colour of mourning so you could pray for missing persons or the bereaved, or those who are sad because they have hurt God or someone close to them and find it hard to be forgiven. The table itself also leads us to think about hospitality and our own meals. You could thank God for communion, and also for feeding us in family meals at home, especially at times of celebration.

If you have a cross...

Perhaps there is a cross, or more than one cross. Do any of them have a special story attached? Some crosses are put in places to remind us of people who died in World War 1. You could use this as a stimulus to think about areas of conflict in the world today and to pray a prayer for peace.

You can also use the cross as an opportunity to remind people of what Christ did for us, and to give thanks. If there is a figure of Christ on the cross, you could draw attention to some aspect of the figure, for example the crown of thorns or the nails. You could remind people of how much love Christ had for us. If the cross is a Celtic cross and has a circle in it, you could include a short extract from Romans 8 about creation waiting for redemption, adding that the cross has a circle in it as a promise that Christ will redeem all creation for us. We will have a new heaven and a new earth – a particularly important promise at the moment when we have so many worries about global warming.

If you have a lectern or reading stand...

Is it plain or decorated? Is there a Bible on it? If there is, encourage people to look up a short passage, such as John 3:16 or Psalm 23 or Christ's command to his disciples in John 15:12,13. Perhaps you could include a few options so that people get the feeling of using the Bible and turning the pages to look something up.

If you have a pulpit...

Is there a pulpit? Is it plain or decorated? Is there any inscription on it? Sometimes pulpits have carvings of an eagle, a man, a lion and an ox upon them – symbols of the writers of the four Gospels. The word 'Gospel' means good news. Perhaps you could pray for those who give good news today, such as those who try to bring comfort in difficult situations such as hospital chaplains.

If you have chairs or pews...

Are they decorated or plain? Sometimes they have gothic patterns on them which might remind people of monasteries, which could lead you to pray for religious communities today: not just monks, but prayer groups, home groups, and anywhere people gather and support one another. Or the pews may have carvings of leaves or animals on them, which may lead you to pray for the planet and those who care for creation.

If you have kneelers, cushions or curtains...

What patterns are on them? Do they inspire you to pray for something?

If you have carpet...

Is there a carpet on the floor? Is it a red carpet? This might inspire you to pray for those in the public gaze such as film actors, but you can also link it to the fact that Christ is a very important person, and that we can also see him in other people and should love and serve them like VIPs too.

If you have cleaning materials or Sunday school equipment tucked away in a cupboard...
This could lead you to pray for those who serve others selflessly by cleaning or by helping to teach the children.

When you have finished writing your prayer trail, print it out onto sheets or fold it into a little booklet. Have a time when a small group of you can pray through the trail and take it for a 'test run'; then leave it available at the back of your church for visitors to use.

43 Text blessings

Normally we tell people to turn off their mobile phones during services, but for this activity you tell people to turn them on instead!

Resources
You will need: some people with mobile phones who are willing to give out their numbers; pieces of scrap paper; pencils.

Method
Invite people to get into groups of two or three, each group having one person with a phone. That person should write their phone number on a small corner of the scrap paper, tear it off and give it to someone else in a different part of the room.

When this has been done, have a short period of silence and listening to God, when people can pray that God will inspire them with particularly apt prayers. Then use the pieces of paper to compose a prayer of encouragement or blessing. Remember that you only have 160 characters to play with, so the prayer has to be short. If you wish, discuss it with the other members of your group. When you have finished composing your prayer of encouragement, get one member of the group to text it to the number you have. Soon you'll hear ringtones all over the church as people receive their prayers of encouragement.

44 Lectio divina

'Lectio divina' simply means 'divine reading'. It is a meditative way of reading the Bible in which we pray over the text and ponder or chew over the meaning for an extended period of time. It is a very old technique of Bible study which has been practised for over a thousand years. The traditional way to do it is on your own, devoting an hour or more to it, but doing it as a group can also be very valuable. Sometimes it can quite naturally lead into discussion. If you choose a well known passage, you will be surprised at how much new information comes out.

Resources
You will need: pens or pencils; a whiteboard or flip chart; a Bible, or a Bible passage printed out – ideally with a lot of space around it for people to use to scribble notes or thoughts alongside the text.

Method
First pray that God's Holy Spirit will come, inspire and speak to and through your group as they study and pray together. Then ask someone to read the passage carefully, with everyone following it on their own copy. Pause for a while to let the words sink in, then invite a different reader to read the passage again. Then pause once more for a few minutes. Now ask people if any word or phrase particularly struck them. If it did, ask them to ponder it, to chew it over, to repeat it in their mind, and to try to understand what God is saying to them through that word or phrase. Give this process some time.

After an extended time of silent meditation, invite the group to feed back anything that has struck them. Then ponder this for a while. Invite people to share any further insights they have about those words.

You could then move into discussion, starting with a relevant question. For example, in the feeding of the five thousand in Mark 6, someone may have chosen the word 'solitary' as seeming to have special significance for them. Why was the place solitary? Listen to, and collect everyone's ideas. You may wish to do this on a whiteboard or flip chart. Then invite people to see if there are any insights they could apply to their lives: What is a solitary place for me? How can I get rest?

Then choose another word. Come up with a question about it, and see what happens. Another example from the passage might be 'late'. Why did they stay so late? Explore the answers. That might lead to a further question: What makes us linger somewhere?

When you have finished your time of discussion, move into prayer once more. Ask God to show you the lessons he wants you to learn and how to apply them to your lives. Is there anything you need to change or do differently? Finally, finish by giving thanks for the new lessons that you have been taught.

45 Speed praying

(with thanks to Ian Birkinshaw)

This prayer is loosely based on the idea of speed dating! But thankfully you don't have to rate the prayers in the way that you have to rate the potential dates you meet!

Resources

You will need: photocopies of the **Speed praying prompt** below; a bell, a watch alarm or another type of time signal; pens or pencils; paper.

Speed praying prompt

... if two of you on earth agree about anything you ask for, it will be done for you by my Father in heaven. For where two or three come together in my name, there am I with them (Matthew 18:19,20).

Praise – something you would like to praise God for

Request – something you need help with

A not-yet Christian – the name of someone you would like to meet Jesus

Your work – some aspect of your work life you are worried about

External concern – a concern from the wider world

Resources – something you need, either physically or spiritually

---

Method

Actually, you can do this prayer activity with no resources whatsoever, but it is sometimes hard to think about what your prayer needs are under time pressure, so it is useful to have a piece of paper with headings on it, as given in the **Speed praying prompt**.

Give out the prompt papers and give people time to think, pray and write down their prayer needs. Divide your group in two, forming two concentric circles. Everyone in the inner circle will pray about the first item on their piece of paper and the people facing them in the outer circle are invited to say prayers or words of agreement such as, 'Yes, Lord!' or 'Amen' or to echo the prayer in short phrases – in other words, to 'agree' with them in prayer.

Someone needs to time the prayers, allowing one minute and then ringing the bell. When the bell rings, the outer circle moves one place clockwise, but the inner circle stays where it is. Then invite the person on the inside to pray about the second item on their piece of paper. When all the needs have been prayed for, swap places so that the outer circle becomes the inner circle, and begin again. This time the new inner circle prays, and the new outer circle agrees with them. Stop when everyone's needs have been prayed for.

Tried & tested

66 Ideally you need at least 12 people for this activity, but you can do it with less – it just means that you pray with the same person more often. We first did this activity at our weekly church staff meeting and everyone felt really encouraged by being prayed for in this way. 99

46 Mount Doom

Resources
You will need: a safe place to light a fire, preferably outside; a mountain cone constructed from wire or bricks or dark coloured foil or alternatively use a metal pot surrounded by materials to make it look like a volcano; A4 sheets of gold or yellow paper; paperclips; pens or pencils; metal tongs.

Method
Be very safety conscious with this activity. Have a fire extinguisher close by just in case it's needed. It's a good idea to appoint a 'minder' to watch the fire and check that people are not getting too close. During the outside activity, if any 'rings' miss 'Mount Doom', get the fire minder to rescue them with metal tongs.

Read the story of the temptations in the desert from Luke 4:1-15. You may also wish to read a short extract from Tolkien's *The Lord of the Rings*. Choose one of the sections particularly focusing on the ring's ability to tempt the ring holder to exert power.

After this, encourage people to think about what their temptations to power might be. Jesus was tempted to misuse his power by ruling over all the kingdoms of the world in a selfish way, which would have meant not submitting to the Father. We, too, are tempted at one time or another to control others, to do things our way rather than God's way, to dominate others.

Next, invite people to write some of those temptations on a piece of paper and, if they wish to, add a prayer of confession for times when they have misused their power over others. Reassure people that nothing they write will be read by anyone else. Afterwards, the pieces of paper should be folded in half along their length, twisted into a ring shape and pinned with a paperclip.

Encourage everyone to go outside and cast their rings into 'Mount Doom' as a way of saying sorry to God for the times they have misused power. Close with a prayer which assures people of God's forgiveness and love.

Tried & tested

66 We did this prayer activity during Lent, when the Bible readings were focusing particularly on Jesus' temptation in the desert. You could do it as part of an Ash Wednesday service. Later in the service you could carefully use the cooled ash from the fire to make the sign of the cross on one another's foreheads as a sign of sorrow for sins. 99

47 Letting go

Resources

You will need: a paddling pool, pond or large bowl of water; some small, attractive polished stones or pebbles of the sort you get from garden centres; a half-erected tent (optional).

Method

Put your half-erected tent in the centre of your worship place as a visual aid. Read the story of the transfiguration from Matthew 17:1–9. Peter wanted to put up a shelter to 'bottle the moment', as it were. Yet sometimes we have to let go to allow something new to happen.

Invite people to ask God: Is there anything I need to let go of? Then allow people, in their own time, to come to the pool and take a pebble. While they hold it, ask them to let that pebble symbolise the thing they want to let go of, and to drop it in the water, watching the ripples grow and die away. While they watch the ripples, they can ask God to make them aware of the new things that are going to happen as a result of letting go of the old thing. If you have a large congregation you may want to set up two or three pools around the building.

It will be helpful to have some people available to pray with anyone feeling they need extra support in their struggle to let something go.

48 Singing prayers

Many Christians look terrified at the idea of chanting prayers, yet there are many easy ways to do this and it can be very meaningful. This activity is one that we have learned from Orthodox Christians, using the Psalms, and we have made it our own. It is very simple to teach. The wonderful thing is that once people have tried chanting, they realise that it really is a lovely way to pray the Psalms.

Resources

You will need: the words of some psalms displayed using a data projector; a good singer or a small group of singers to give a good strong lead; a musical backing track on CD (optional).

> **Note:** There are a number of places on the Internet where you can get easily 'singable' versions of the Psalms. I recommend the Church of England site: (http://www.cofe.anglican.org/worship/liturgy/commonworship/texts/psalter/psalter.html). As for the backing track, there are many chillout dance tracks that are suitable, such as 'Smokebelch II' by The Sabres of Paradise or a number of tracks by Moby or Chicane. Basically, any kind of backing music that is mostly on one chord and doesn't radically change key usually works. Alternatively, if you have a bouncy youth group you might decide to try this over a loud trance techno track, which has lots of energy. Or you could use live guitar backing, experimenting with different chords and rhythms to give the music more interest.

Method

Teach your group three-note chanting. The aim is to sing all the words on the first line on one note, then sing all the words on the second line on another note until they reach the second-to-last syllable and then go back up to the first note again. If you have a data projector you could colour code the syllable on which people change note to make it more obvious. You could have your small singing group or soloist alternate the verses of the psalms with everyone else to vary the musical texture.

At the top of the next page is an example of the chant written down in musical notation, using the beginning of Psalm 150 as an example. Don't feel you have to stick to this key; sing it in any key you like, and use the rhythm of the text rather than a strict musical rhythm. Sing it as you would normally say it.

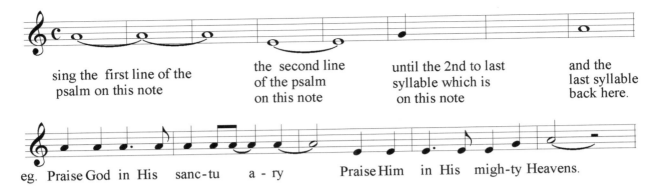

sing the first line of the psalm on this note

the second line of the psalm on this note

until the 2nd to last syllable which is on this note

and the last syllable back here.

eg. Praise God in His sanc-tu a - ry Praise Him in His migh-ty Heavens.

After you have practised, you could add your choice of backing track. As well as the Psalms, other prayers from the Bible can also be set to music. It's a great way of memorising Bible text.

49 Chains

Resources
You will need: a large collection of white and coloured pipe cleaners, at least one for each member of the group but preferably more. These are widely available from craft shops.

Method
Make your pipe cleaners into the links of a chain, joined together so that the length stretches across part of the building. Read a passage of the Bible about slavery and freedom, such as Romans 6:15–23. Then invite people to come up and unpick a link of the chain and, as they do so, to pray for someone who is a slave today. This could be someone who is literally a slave – physical slavery still being a tragic reality even in the twenty-first century. Or it could be someone who is enslaved to an addiction. Or someone they know who feels trapped by their circumstances.

Ask people to take their pipe cleaner and shape it into something that symbolises freedom or new life, as they continue to pray.

50 Saintly mirrors

Resources
You will need: some tiny mirror tiles (mosaic ones work best); some magnetic tape (available from craft shops); a metal object such as a cake tin; a desk lamp or spotlight; background music or a worship song about being the light of the world (optional); a whiteboard or OHP.

Method
Cut the magnetic tape into little squares and stick onto the back of the mirror tiles, which enables you to stick the tiles onto metal objects and reposition or remove them whenever you wish.

Begin the prayer activity by reading a Bible passage such as Matthew 5:14–16, which is about Jesus' followers being the 'light of the world'. Explain that the light we have comes from Jesus. As holy people spend time with God, they begin to reflect his light and to shine it into dark corners, as mirrors reflect the light of a lamp. God calls all of us to be holy, and to reflect the light of Christ into other people's lives.

Give out the mirror tiles. Warn people to be careful as they handle them; sometimes the edges may be rough. Display three questions for people to think and pray about:

*   Who has shone the light of Christ into my life and been an inspiration to me? Thank God for those people now.

- How can I shine more? Am I hiding my light? Am I spending enough time with God in order to reflect his light? Are there other things I could do to help me shine more?

- Sometimes other things get in the way of us shining. Sin or fear maybe. Is there anything about which you need to say sorry to God? Ask God to shine in your life and help you to be a light to others.

After praying, invite people to place their mirror tile on the metal object as a sign that they are giving themselves to God and want to shine with his light. You could play or sing an appropriate song about light while this is happening. When everyone has placed their tiles on the metal object, switch on the desk lamp or spotlight and point it at the object. Hopefully this should make sparkling spots of light appear on the ceiling as the tiles reflect the light, the effect being something like a disco mirror ball. Offer a prayer of thanks that Christ gives us his light to share.

Tried & tested

We did this prayer activity at an All Saints service that we held in York Minster. It is especially effective at night. We used a tall metal cake tin that looked something like a crown and when we had all put our mirror tiles on it, we placed the 'crown of light' at the foot of the cross. We used the song, 'We shine in the light of your love, like the moon reflects the sun', by The Tribe in LA. This seems to have been withdrawn from sale, although the Church of the Apostles in Seattle have covered it in their album 'Laudamus'.

51 Parasols of protection

Resources

You will need: some coloured paper cocktail parasols (one per person); Blu-Tack or Plasticine; a large world map, preferably laminated; a desk lamp or spotlight.

Method

Display the world map with your light source shining onto it from one side. Invite people to come up to the map and pray for areas of the world experiencing conflict and needing God's peace. Think about the people there who need protection from the bombs and bullets or protection from other things such as starvation or bad harvests. Each person in turn places their parasol in such a way that its shadow falls on the place you are all praying for, securing it with Blu-Tack.

Finally, conclude with a prayer of thanks for all the times we have been protected by God when we have been in fearful or difficult situations.

52 Harvest for the world

Resources

You will need: wild flowers such as daisies, buttercups, dandelions, nice grasses; several vases with water in them; a portable CD player and the track 'Harvest for the world' (optional).

Note: This standard, which goes 'All babies together/ Everyone a seed/ Half of us are satisfied/ Half of us in need...' has been put out by many singers. At Visions we particularly like the version by Caroline Henderson.

Method

Before the service starts, put the vases around your communion table or at the foot of a large cross.

Introduce your prayer activity by telling people that this is a time to think about those people you would love God to gather into his Church – people who don't yet know Jesus, or people who have fallen away from their faith for some reason. Then encourage everyone to take a flower for each person they want to pray for. If you have wild flowers growing in the church grounds, you could all go out and actually pick them then and there. Otherwise, have some bunches available. Play the music track and ask people to put their flowers in the vases as a sign of hope and of placing those people and their situations into God's hands.

Tried & tested

66 We used ox-eye daisies as there were huge numbers of these growing in our churchyard. We did this activity at a communion service one summer. It was wonderful to go outside in the sunshine and 99 gather flowers during the service.

53 The cross

Resources

You will need: copies of the script from page 77.

Method

This is a prayer based on the sign of the cross, which is one of the oldest physical prayers used by Christians. Sometimes people pray the prayer without thinking or superstitiously. Here we slow everything down, enabling people to give it some thought.

There are a few different variations on the prayer. Orthodox Christians make the cross with three fingers, symbolising the Trinity, and from right to left.

Using the script, repeat the prayer two or three times, and then without the directions.

54 Inside out

Resources

You will need: the clothing that people are wearing! This works well at times of year when you can expect people to be wearing a jacket, coat, jumper, gloves or hat. It also helps to have a warm building so that people don't mind taking their jackets or jumpers off!

Method

Sometimes people's lives get turned inside out. Sometimes it is due to a terrible experience. But sometimes God turns people's lives inside out in a really good way.

Invite people to take off their jumpers (or alternatively coats, hat or gloves) and turn them inside out.

As they do so, invite them to think about people whose lives have been turned inside out this week. Perhaps they know someone who has lost someone they love; or someone who has received an unwelcome diagnosis of illness; or someone who had some other kind of really bad news such as redundancy. Then pass the jumpers around. Everyone prays for the owner of the jumper they are holding. After praying, each person turns the jumper they are holding the right way round and prays that God will turn the owner's life inside out in a good way, that they will draw closer to God and feel his presence beside them, making them whole where they have been wounded. Finally, return the jumpers to the owners with a word of blessing.

55 Shining talents

Resources

You will need: a large lamp or candle; a packet of tea lights, one for each person; a collection of tea light holders – you can buy beautiful holders or you can make your own using jam jars covered in coloured cellophane; long matches or ordinary matches and spills.

Method

Begin your time of prayer with a lamplighting prayer such as this one, which is a version of the Phos Hilaron, one of the oldest Christian prayers:

> O joyful flame!
> From the Father's perfect glory,
> You came to set our lives alight.
> Holy, precious Christ,
> You are the flame within our hearts.
>
> The sun is setting
> And the lamps are coming on
> And once again
> We thank the Father and the Son
> And the Spirit, ever One.
>
> You are worthy through all time.
> We sing your praise and raise our voices.
> Son of God, you give us life,
> And all creation speaks your story.

Invite people to take a tea light and holder and light it from the flame of the larger lamp. Ask people to imagine that their lamps represent the gifts and talents that they have been given by God. As they hold their lamps for a while, they can thank God for the gifts he has given them.

Next, invite people to blow out the lamp. As they do so, they should pray for someone who has been prevented from realising a talent, or someone who can no longer use a talent through illness, injury or old age.

Then invite people to gather at the front and relight someone else's lamp. During this time they should pray that God will show everyone how best to use and develop one another's talents.

56 Prayer tunnels

Resources

You will need: nothing special apart from a number of people willing to pray!

Method

Gather people willing to act as a 'prayer tunnel', arranged in two lines facing one another. This is one of the times when having an old-fashioned church with pews is quite useful because people can lean against the pew ends and form two parallel lines. Then ask them to stretch up their hands in prayer, reaching out at an angle to the person opposite but not joining hands, so as to allow people walking through the 'tunnel' enough room.

Everyone else can walk through the tunnel slowly, thinking about their current prayer needs. Those forming the tunnel are invited to pray for those who are walking past them, either silently or aloud. When the people being prayed for have finished walking through the tunnel, some of them can form a tunnel for the first tunnel group to walk through, so that everyone is prayed for.

A variation on this is to use a technique similar to some ceilidh dances, when people join the end of the tunnel as they finish walking through.

Another variation can be used in the context of someone leaving the church: perhaps they are going on a missionary trip or leaving the town to start a new job. Call the person being sent out up to the front of the church, where they can be interviewed about their new role. Then invite the whole congregation to turn so that they form two groups, each facing the other across the central aisle and then you can literally 'send out' the person, who walks slowly between the people, as they pray for them.

57 Bitter, sweet, salt and sour

This prayer activity links the four main tastes to the four main types of prayer: adoration, confession, intercession and thanksgiving.

Resources
You will need: four bowls – one filled with bitter herbs such as parsley or thyme; one filled with salt water; one filled with honey; one filled with some sour fruit such as grapefruit segments.

Method
The bowls are passed around and people can taste the contents if they wish. When they receive the bitter bowl, invite them to pray prayers of confession. You can link this to the book of Exodus, when the Hebrews ate bitter herbs to remind them of the bitterness of slavery. In our case, the herbs remind us of the bitterness of the slavery of sin.

When people receive the salt water, ask them to pray for those who are crying salty tears today through illness, grief, pain or loss. When people receive the bowl of honey, invite them to pray a prayer of adoration to the God whose laws are sweeter than honey. Finally, when people receive the sour fruit bowl, invite them to give thanks to God for all the challenges he gives us, that he will enable us to meet even the difficulties of life with a loving servant heart.

58 The empty chair

Resources
You will need: a small dining table (or anything that will look like a dining table by having a cloth spread on it); three chairs; knives, forks, plates and glasses; dining table candles and matches (optional); a black permanent OHP pen; some background music (optional); some surgical spirit or cheap alcohol to use afterwards.

Method
Lay the table with two places as you would do normally for a meal, leaving a third place with a chair but no place setting. Then, using the OHP pen, write on the two plates the thoughts you imagine people may be having when facing an empty chair at the dinner table.

For example, you could write: 'I miss her... I could talk to her about anything... she always knew what to do when things went wrong... ' Or: 'I miss him... he told the best bedtime stories... he always played the most fun games... I always felt safe in his arms... '

You could play a song about grief or loss, or a song of intercession, as people come and walk past the table. Depending on the size of the group, and what time is available, you could invite people to sit at one or other place for a short while, imagining themselves in that person's place, and praying for those who have lost someone. You can finish the time of prayer by lighting the candles on the table and praying together.

Give people the option of praying with others after the service if they would like to.

You can remove the OHP ink from the plate with the alcohol. Be sure to wash up the plates properly afterwards.

Tried & tested

 We have found that this prayer activity is particularly poignant near Christmas, or during November, when many churches hold services for the recently bereaved.

59 Broken things

Resources

You will need: a collection of broken items – anything from a torn map to a dead house plant, a broken plate, a damaged radio or mobile; a medicine bottle; a small table; a wooden cross, small enough to be passed around.

Method

Introduce all the items and talk about what they might represent. The torn map might stand for our broken world; the dead house plant, our damaged ecosystems. The broken plate could represent broken family relationships. The radio or mobile could stand for damaged communication between us and God, and us and other people. The medicine bottle represents our broken bodies. You can be inventive and find other things to represent broken promises, corrupted government and so on.

Then pass around all the items apart from the cross, and invite people to pray for the situations that come to mind, silently or aloud, alone or in groups. Remind people to be careful of any sharp edges.

Finally, place them all in a jumble on the table. Pass the small cross around the group, reminding people that on the cross Christ's body was broken to make us whole and save our broken world. Ask people to say prayers of hope and thanks when they receive the cross. Afterwards, place the cross in the centre of all the other objects as a promise that all these things will be redeemed.

Tried & tested

 We first got the idea for this prayer activity out of necessity, when we discovered that one of the inflatable globes we used during services was broken. We realised that we could still use the broken globe to pray for our broken world, and that led to us thinking about other broken items too.

60 Rings of promise

Many people at Easter like to remember and renew the promises they made at their baptism. We wanted to do this in a way that used the symbols of water and light together, but without the light being extinguished. We came up with the idea of using glow sticks, which you can order in packets of mixed colours quite cheaply through the Internet.

Resources

You will need: a paddling pool, baptistry or font – ideally low enough so that people can see the glowing rings; glow sticks; copies of a promise script – you can either use the words provided below or you can use your own denominational form of promises. Alternatively, you may prefer people to say something personal and improvised.

Method

Dim the lights and gather people around your pool. Set the scene for a time of remembering and renewing the promises we made to follow Christ at our baptism.

Give out the glow sticks but tell people not to light them yet. Distribute the promise words and encourage everyone to join in, following every question with the response: I do.

Promises

Do you reject the devil and all rebellion against God?

And all the deceit and corruption of evil?

And hatred, whatever form it takes?

And all the glitz and glamour of wrong choices?

And the selfishness that hurts all creation so much?

And the things that separate us from God and our friends?

And the excuses that stop us from doing good works?

And the laziness that stops us from fulfilling God's plans?

Do you turn to Christ, the source of our life?

Will you follow Christ, wherever he leads?

Will you listen to Christ, whenever he speaks?

Will you serve Christ, as he leads you into life?

When you have finished your promises, invite people to snap and twist their glow sticks into rings or bracelets. They can then throw their bracelets into the pool and then choose another one of a different colour. This is a reminder that, with Christ, life is never quite the same again. We are not the same people we were before we became Christians. Finally invite people to put on their bracelets as a sign of new life and their role in shining in a dark world.

61 Prayer beads

The wonderful thing about prayer beads is how very tactile they are. Sometimes holding something while you pray can really help with concentration. Different Christian traditions have evolved different ways of using prayer beads. You may not be comfortable with some of these techniques, yet there are always ways of adapting prayer activities to create something that feels relevant and comfortable to your group.

Resources

You will need: thin black elastic; beads of different colours that fit on the elastic – either get these from craft shops or buy cheap necklaces from charity shops and break them up for the beads; a needle for threading the beads onto the elastic; some small plastic tubs.

Method

Divide your beads by colour among the plastic tubs. Think of something that you would like that colour of bead to symbolise and write it on a small sign beside each tub. Some examples of what you could choose are given below. Much will depend on the beads you have available.

Cut the black elastic into lengths that will go around most people's wrists when knotted, distribute them and invite people to thread the beads themselves, in any order, praying for different situations as guided by the colours as they do so.

When they are finished, ask people to knot their elastic into a bracelet to wear or carry around to remind them to pray for these situations throughout the week.

Examples of labels:

Black for mourning – pray for someone or some situation which is causing people to grieve.

Red for rage – pray for someone who is full of rage at the moment; maybe they are angry because of not being forgiving or because of unresolved relationship problems.

Blue for rivers, roads and skies – pray for any you know who are travelling, whether on the pale blue of the sea, the midnight blue tarmac of the motorways, or the silver blue shimmer of a train.

Green for new life – pray for those who are starting a new job or school, or those who have just become Christians.

White for angel's wings – pray for those in need of protection, perhaps because they are in a place of danger such as a war zone, or being persecuted for their faith.

Yellow for gold coins and palaces – pray for world leaders and for the rich and powerful in key areas of influence.

Orange for sunset – pray for those who are terminally ill or about to leave behind anything they love.

Brown for sticky mud – pray for people who are in trouble, who have got themselves stuck in a situation and can't find a way out.

Pink for sweet-smelling roses, carnations, marshmallows and candyfloss – thank God for all the sweet experiences he has given you recently, and all the prayers he has answered.

Tried & tested

“ If your church is having a special week of prayer or a mission week, you could create beads that remind people to pray for different aspects of that event. Or you could create a set that remind people to pray for different countries, perhaps based on the colours used in their national flags. ”

62 American prayer beads

I discovered American prayer beads when I was on placement with the Church of the Apostles in Seattle. Most people in the community had a set of beads, which they kept in their pockets or attached to their belt or in their car. They used the beads to help them pray, or to remind them to pray. This form of beads was invented by the Rev Lynn Bauman in the 1980s as a sort of cross between Catholic and Orthodox prayer beads and seems to have become popular in many American churches.

Resources

You will need for each person: 28 small beads; seven larger beads – or beads of a different colour; a small cross pendant or cross-shaped bead; some nylon wire, embroidery silk, or string; glue (optional).

Method

Start by cutting your thread to a size big enough for all your beads, plus a little extra in case of miscalculations. Then thread your little cross on the wire to become the central point. Next thread one of the larger beads over both wires, not just one. After this, split the two threads once more and thread another large bead on each side of the wire. After this, on each side of the string, thread seven small beads and another large one, then seven more and another large bead. Finally, tie the thread together at the top with a secure knot. If you can, hide this knot under one of the large beads. You may wish to secure the knot with a little dab of glue.

Hopefully you will end up with something like the picture here.

Once you have made your prayer beads, there are many different ways to use them. Below are a few that I have found helpful, some of which echo prayers used by the early Christians. But you may wish to experiment and come up with some new ideas that you can share with others.

Variation 1

Hold the cross and pray:

'In the name of the holy and undivided Trinity – Father, Son and Holy Spirit',

and then, holding the next large bead, pray:

'Holy God, holy and strong, holy and immortal one, have mercy upon us.'

Repeat this same prayer for each of the following large beads. On each of the little beads, pray:

'Jesus Christ, Son of God, have mercy on me, a sinner'.

Variation 2

A variation of this is to pray on the cross and the large beads as before, but on the seven small beads to pray:

Jesus Christ, Son of God, have mercy on our street...
Jesus Christ, Son of God, have mercy on our town...
Jesus Christ, Son of God, have mercy on our country...
Jesus Christ, Son of God, have mercy on our culture...
Jesus Christ, Son of God, have mercy on our world...
Jesus Christ, Son of God, have mercy on our church...
Jesus Christ, Son of God, have mercy on me... I have hurt you.

Variation 3

You could assign each bead to a street in your area, or a church in your city that you would like to pray for. Potentially, you have 21 different places or people that you can regularly pray for using the beads.

Variation 4

Some people have taken three different Celtic prayers and assigned different beads to those. Or you may wish to use the beads in the way that Orthodox Christians do, praying on every bead the Jesus prayer:

'Jesus Christ, Son of God, have mercy on me, a sinner.'

63 Rosary prayers

It has been interesting to see that standard rosary beads have become fashion items in recent years and people who aren't Christians have been wearing them. If you do want to buy some, here are some ideas of prayer activities you can do with them. Obviously, you could also adapt any of the ideas from **Prayer beads** and **American prayer beads** on the previous pages.

The rosary and the Lord's Prayer

The beads can be used to pray the Lord's Prayer (Matthew 6:9–13) in a meditative way, allowing the meaning of the words to sink deep into you. After a while, you will know which line of the prayer you are on simply by which bead you are holding. This liberates you to think about – for example – places where you would like God's kingdom to come.

Begin on the little medal at the join in the beads. On the medal and on each single bead, pray;

'For the kingdom the power and the glory are yours, now and forever.'

On each set of ten little beads, pray the Lord's Prayer this way:

1   Our Father in heaven...
2   hallowed be your name...
3   your kingdom come...
4   your will be done...
5   on earth as in heaven...
6   give us today our daily bread...
7   forgive us our sins...
8   as we forgive those who sin against us...
9   lead us not into temptation...
10   but deliver us from evil.

An evangelical rosary

Rosary beads were originally designed to be used as a tool to meditate on salvation history while praying. Because the original rosary was very Mary-focused it fell out of use in England at the Reformation, yet in recent years a number of Protestants have experimented with more Christ-centred versions of the prayer.

This one can be a little tricky to master at first, for when people pray the rosary they are really doing three things at once: using their hands on the beads, saying the prayers with their mouths and using their minds to meditate on scripture.

Start at the large triangular medal and use it as if it was a single bead. On each single bead, including this one, pray:

'Glory be to the Father and to the Son and to the Holy Spirit, as it was in the beginning, is now and ever shall be, world without end, Amen.'

Travel clockwise around the beads. When you reach a set of ten beads, look up the appropriate Bible text (listed below) and read it. Then pray the Lord's Prayer ten times – once each bead – using the prayer as 'time keeping' while you meditate on this incident in the Bible.

Read the Bible text just before you pray each set of prayers – sometimes called a decade because there are ten beads – and then use the time to imagine what that incident was like. You may like to create an interaction between the Lord's Prayer and the incident. So, for example, you can reflect on how God's kingdom is coming in this incident; how God's will is being done on earth through it, and so on. If you are doing this as a group, perhaps you'd like to then spend some time reflecting back your thoughts in discussion, before moving on to another incident in Jesus' life.

There are 15 events in biblical history to think and pray about here. To do the whole set you would normally go around the beads three times as there are normally only five decades on each rosary, unless you have one of the extra long ones used by some nuns and monks.

The 15 biblical events:

The annunciation of Jesus' birth (Luke 1:26–38)

Mary visits Elizabeth (Luke 1:39–56)

The birth of Jesus (Luke 2:1–14)

Jesus is presented in the temple (Luke 2:21–38)

Jesus visits the temple as a boy (Luke 2:41–49)

Jesus prays in the Garden of Gethsemane (Luke 22:39–46)

Jesus is whipped (Mark 15:14,15)

Jesus is crowned with thorns (Mark 15:16–20)

Jesus carries his cross (Luke 23:26–32)

Jesus is crucified (Luke 23:32–43)

Jesus rises from the dead (John 20:1–18)

Jesus ascends into heaven (Acts 1:7–11)

The Spirit comes at Pentecost (Acts 2:1–13)

Jesus will return at the end of the world (Matthew 24:3–8, 27–31)

The new Jerusalem (Revelation 21:1–7)

64 Bandages

Resources

You will need: bandages cut into small lengths (or strips of old white cloth that look like bandages); something to wrap the bandages around – perhaps a communion rail if you have one, or a cross, or the legs of the communion table; safety pins; background music or a song on the theme of Christ the healer (optional).

Method

Give out a piece of bandage and a safety pin to everyone. Introduce the activity by reading (and perhaps commenting on) James 5:14–16, about the prayer of faith healing the sick.

Invite your group to think of people they know who are sick or suffering and take time to pray for them. After praying, they could go to the front and pin their bandage on the cross (or whatever you are using) as a way of giving this person to God.

Tried & tested

 If you want to use this in the context for praying for sick children, you could use teddy bears to pin the bandages onto.

Script: Umbrellas

Look at the umbrellas.

Umbrellas come in all different shapes and sizes, but one purpose they share is to protect you from the rain. When we step out into new things, it can be scary... especially if we are stepping out of our comfort zone and going to new places and meeting new people. But God will protect us. In Isaiah 43, God reassures us about this protection:

> Fear not, for I have redeemed you;
> I have summoned you by name; you are mine.
> When you pass through the waters,
> I will be with you;
> and when you pass through the rivers,
> they will not sweep over you.
> When you walk through the fire,
> you will not be burned;
> the flames will not set you ablaze.
> For I am the LORD, your God,
> the Holy One of Israel, your Saviour.

The things that frighten you right now will not last for ever... but God is always with you.

Script: Pearls of wisdom

Think for a moment about those wise people who have taught you the most. Write some of their names on your triangle now...

Remind yourself what it was about them that made you consider them wise. Pray for them now... and thank God for what they taught you...

Now begin to think about yourself, and what you need to become wiser...

James says that to be truly wise we need to be submissive, impartial and sincere. We need to be willing to learn from others... we need to not let ambition blind us to the truth...

Now write a list on your triangle of some of those things you would like God to help you with... so you can become wiser.

Script: Rags to riches

Isaiah 64:6 and 9 say:

> All of us have become like one who is unclean,
> and all our righteous acts are like filthy rags;
> we all shrivel up like a leaf,
> and like the wind our sins sweep us away.
>
> Do not be angry beyond measure, O Lord;
> do not remember our sins forever.
> Oh, look upon us, we pray,
> for we are all your people.

Invite people to take a piece of rag from the collection.

Look carefully at your piece of rag. Once it was a beautiful piece of cloth being woven on a large loom, bright and full of promise. Now it is old and frayed. Perhaps there are things in your life that feel a bit like that these days. Perhaps there was a dream of doing something beautiful for God that didn't work out because you didn't persevere with it. Or some good deed that you meant to do but never quite got around to. Or maybe you meant to be pure and good this week, but somehow you got tempted into going the wrong way.

Think for a minute about some of the things that come to mind when you look at your rag... things you want to say sorry to God for... things you did which you wish you hadn't... things you wish you had done and never got around to. Then, when you are ready, tie your cloth to the cross, as a sign that you are sorry and need God's forgiveness.

Wait for everyone to tie their rags to the cross.

In Isaiah 61 we read these words of reassurance:

The Spirit of the Sovereign Lord is on me,
> because the Lord has anointed me
> to preach good news to the poor.
> He has sent me to bind up the brokenhearted,
> to proclaim freedom for the captives
> and release from darkness for the prisoners ...
>
> to bestow on them a crown of beauty
> instead of ashes,
> the oil of gladness
> instead of mourning,
> and a garment of praise
> instead of a spirit of despair.
> They will be called oaks of righteousness,
> a planting of the Lord
> for the display of his splendour.

Script: Christmas meditation

Let's put away the worries and stresses that Christmas so often brings... the anxieties that get in the way of worshipping God. Let's begin to focus on the meaning at the very heart of Christmas.

Stand up... shake yourself... stretch... then sit down... make yourself comfortable... relax... close your eyes if you wish...

Now imagine... imagine that you are a traveller. You have come a very long way... all the way from Africa... carrying a small quantity of precious, fragrant burning resin. You have ridden for hundreds of miles on horseback till your thighs are aching and sore. You have travelled on foot too, till your back aches and your feet throb, because sometimes the territory was too forbidding or too steep to stay mounted. You are now in a strange country. It is night... and the nights are cold.

Yes, since you began climbing higher into the hills, the temperature has been dropping. It feels like you are on the roof of the world here. Though it was pleasantly hot at noon, now at night it is much colder... colder than you have ever known. There is frost on the ground. You have heard tales of this white powdery stuff that covers the sand where the dew has dropped, but no one has ever told you what it felt like before... how the frost bites at your fingers... how the cold wind cuts into your face... how your knees ache in the middle of the night with only a flimsy tent to protect you.

You wrap your thick, woollen travelling cloak tighter around you and you continue searching...

You feel scared and lost... very lost. Although you have travelling companions and a servant nearby, you know how vulnerable you are in a strange place, with different customs. And this place is under military rule. Troops have been marching past you at regular intervals on the journey. Sometimes you have heard jeers and shouts from these passing cohorts... and the fear is always at the back of your mind. Your companions feel the same. What if they turned on us? We could never fight against them, there are too many of them. But, so far, they have not. Their officers took command... told them to march faster. They disappeared over the horizon, the soles of their boots drumming rhythmically into the road.

Yet the fear stayed... deep down... and the despair too... and the tiny voice inside telling you that you must be crazy to leave everything you know behind you, just to search.

Because you are searching... looking for a newly born king. Looking for some answers in life, too...

The obvious place to look for a king is in a palace... but the only palace near this place had no children's cries in it. Only a bad tempered ruler who could almost have murdered you on the spot, and a few local priests of the ancient and complex religion they follow in these parts. These holy men directed you six miles to the south. But you aren't really sure who you can trust... the king who asks you to report back to him with the cold steel of a threat in his voice... or the priests who consult their ancient scriptures and give the name of a tiny hamlet miles away from anywhere important.

Your confusion mounts... and the black pit of fear in your stomach grows. Was this long journey all for nothing?

You carry on walking through the night... and now you reach the village. Someone has scrawled the name of the place on a wooden post near a watering trough. The place is riddled with caves... like a giant anthill. You begin to wonder where on earth you should be looking next. But then you gaze into the sky, and, as you gaze, the starlight seems to crystallise through the freezing air, pointing the way to one old family home in particular... a place about as far removed from a palace as you could wish... deeply, deeply ordinary... yet something makes you want to look further. You lift the latch. And smell... not goat dung... but something animal all the same... a cow, and the remains of whatever the cow had for breakfast... the ripe smell makes you cover your nose.

You look around. A scrubbed corner... and in the scrubbed corner, a young woman is lying on a pile of straw.

Pale... as if she has been bleeding... as if she has recently been through a great ordeal. And a man, somewhat older... trying to persuade her to drink some wine from a goatskin.

You hail him. He looks puzzled. You remember just how far you are from home so you try again, not in your native tongue this time but in the rough traders' Greek you have picked up over the years. He replies, falteringly... 'Hail stranger, come in.'

You ask, 'I have come from far away. I am looking for a baby king.'

He points to a feeding trough. Perhaps he is offering food for the horses. You peer inside... and you are shocked. A baby... too purple and wrinkled to be more than a few hours old, tiny and fragile, wrapped in pieces of cloth. You stare straight into the child's eyes, and he seems to stare right back at you, in an unfocused kind of way. You move closer... what do you say?

Pause for prayer.

The baby seems to want to communicate with you. He has no speech as yet, but his eyes bore a message into your very soul. What is he saying to you?

Pause to listen to God.

And now you feel compelled to give the child a gift. You have brought frankincense from your home country for him... but you also want to give him something else. What do you want to give him now... a personal gift between you and him that no one else can see?

Pause for prayer.

Your companions come in too. They pay their respects and give gifts... and then you all leave, after a brief conversation of halting phrases... something tremendously important has happened. You sit and think about what this can all mean... you think about the next step.

Pause to listen to God.

And then you hear singing... strange, ghostly music, which seems to come from the clouds and the frosty air itself... music that's both a song of joy and a lullaby.

Script: Mint

Look at your mint leaf carefully. Admire its beauty... its colour... its shape... the veins... and thank God for it as part of his wonderful creation.

Now rub your leaf... note its fragility... how it bruises... how easily it is crushed...

Pray for those you know who are bruised... either literally bruised by domestic or other violence... or emotionally bruised by rejection or disappointment... or crushed by poverty or hardship...

Now tear your leaf... and, as you do so, pray for those who are torn and divided... think of relationships that have been torn apart... people torn apart internally by conflicting priorities... think of divided countries...

Smell your leaf... savour the scent of the mint rising into your nose... sweet and beautiful, like the scent of our prayers rising to God like incense...

Look once again at the leaf, lying torn and bruised in the palm of your hand... think and pray for our broken world... pray for God to restore our broken creation...

Finally... come and place your leaf in one of the jugs as a sign of offering all your prayers to God in the name of Jesus, who was also torn and broken on our behalf to bring us healing.

Script: White stones

In the book of Revelation, Jesus appears and says to those who live in Pergamum 'Let anyone who has an ear listen to what the Spirit is saying to the churches. To everyone who conquers I will give some of the hidden manna, and I will give a white stone, and on the white stone is written a new name that no one knows except the one who receives it' (Revelation 2:17 NRSV).

Jesus has hard words for the people who lived in Pergamum... they were being led astray and sliding into idol worship...

Think now of some situation where you struggle with compromising... where you find it hard listening to competing voices... perhaps society is telling you acting this way is fine... but Jesus is telling you to follow him... Give that situation to Jesus now... give him all your worries about it... ask for his strength to conquer those worries and stay close to him. 'To everyone who conquers I will give some of the hidden manna, and I will give a white stone...' a white stone, not a black one...

The Greeks voted with stones... white for yes, black for no... Jesus is giving you the white voting-stone of God's 'yes' vote... God wants you... he does not reject you... God has chosen you to be part of his people. Now, in your own time, and if you feel you can, go up to the front of the church and pick a white stone out of the pot. If someone else does not want to go up, volunteer to get a stone for them too. Then, when you all have stones, write the name of the person next to you on the side of the stone with the OHP pen that is being passed around. On the other side, if you feel you know the person well enough, write another name... the name of something you have appreciated about them. It could be 'good listener', 'faithful friend', 'lovely voice', 'nice smile', 'honest'. Even if you've just met your neighbour, there may be something encouraging you can write on the stone. Do this in pairs, making a threesome if you need to so that no one is left out.

When you have finished, give the stones to the person named on them, so that they can be looked at and then taken home.

Script: Living stones

Pick up your stone and hold it carefully. Many stones come from gardens. And that is where we, too, began... in the garden... the paradise of Eden...

But God's utopia is urban... the new Jerusalem. We are going to a city. We cannot go back to the garden. God does not want to rewind history and bring us back to the start.

God does not want annihilation... God wants transformation... heaven... the new Jerusalem... is a city... not a garden.

Why a city? Perhaps because God has incorporated our energy and effort... our inventions and technology... into his plans... gates... walls... foundations... measuring rods and streets...

The incredible, mind-blowing thing is that God does not want to sweep us away. No, God wants to use us to help build the new Jerusalem... the city which also has a tree in it... a healing tree.

Each of us has a stone to lay in that new city. Each of us has a task that God, the architect of the heavenly Jerusalem, has asked us to do...

Some of the tasks God asks of us are huge... some are tiny, but just as important.

So what is the task God is asking me to do? What is he asking you to do?

When you are ready, lay your stone by the side of the river of life which flows through the centre of the heavenly city, making riverbanks as a symbol of offering yourself and that task to God.

Script: Meditation on a stone

Hold your stone, while we think prayerfully about the many incidents where stones appear in the Bible. We could think of the stones that built the temple... the stone that killed Goliath... the stones that killed Stephen... we could think of the cairn that was built when the Israelites crossed the Jordan as God held back the waters... or the stones that Jesus said would cry out if the people stopped shouting 'Hosanna' as he rode into Jerusalem.

What can you do with a stone?

You can throw your stones at a dangerous person, should your definition of 'dangerous' be someone you disagree with. You can beat them till they cry 'Lord Jesus, receive my spirit' and they lie down and die...

You can build them into a house, a temple for God, with carved pomegranates decorating the borders... and know that God will come and visit the structure you have made...

You can stretch up your head and admire the cornerstone at the top... the one that holds all the others together... and know that someone once rejected it... but now it has the highest place...

You can launch your stone within a slingshot and kill a giant warrior... saving a persecuted people. But your stone would then be bloody, even though it saved some lives...

You can lead a spiritually hungry people through a dry and dusty desert and, when their mouths are parched with thirst, strike a stone with your old staff and watch clean water gushing out...

You can build a cairn to remember a great miracle like holding back the Jordan river for travellers to cross...

You could march seven times around stone walls and watch them tumble down... so prisoners can be released and evil rulers deposed...

You can give it to your child, when they ask you for some bread, but you know deep down you wouldn't... because you want them to eat well and grow up beautiful and strong...

You can put your ear next to your stone and listen for its song, knowing that if we stopped our praises, it would cry 'hosanna' to the King...

Your stone can kill, your stone can build, your stone might sing, or might gush water.

The choice is yours. What do you most want to do with your stone?

Script: God's vineyard

A landowner planted a vineyard... the landowner, not me... I am just a tenant. It is God's vineyard... not mine...

In my mind, I imagine looking over the grapes. How are they doing? Are they growing well? Are there grapes that need a little bit of help, or extra loving care? Who comes into my mind as I look at those grapes? I will pray for those people now...

It is God's vineyard... not mine.

What other fruit is the vineyard producing? Paul said the fruit of the Spirit is love, joy, peace, patience, goodness, kindness, gentleness, faithfulness and self-control. Do I see any of these fruits growing in me?

Love... joy... peace... patience... goodness... kindness... gentleness... faithfulness... and self-control...

Do I see any of these fruits growing in other parts of God's vineyard? Who comes to mind when I think of these fruits? I thank God for those people now...

Am I tending my vine? What kinds of things would best help me to grow? Is there anything I need to add, to help my vine grow a little more? How can I do that? Spending more time with God in prayer? Spending more time with God in reading his Word? How can I do that?

Do I need to go out and stretch my faith a little? How can I do that?

The owner of the vineyard is coming...

How do I feel about that? Am I excited? Expectant? Afraid? Why do I feel that way?

Is there anything I want to say to God?

The owner will be asking for the produce at harvest time...

What sort of produce might he want from me? How can I best produce it?

It is God's vineyard... not mine.

Script: Grief transformed

In the darkness, the apostles waited, their lives crushed by grief. Yet, as the first fingers of dawn stretched across the sky, Christ opened his mouth and took his first resurrected breath... Angels rolled away the stone, and he stepped into the sunlight, the Risen One.

The light that was extinguished is now resurrected and transformed... from the bruised and beaten body tortured and wrecked on a tree, he has become the all-powerful Lord of all. Death itself has been kicked in the teeth. And, because he can bring life to the dead, we know that he can transform all our griefs too... everything that we wrote on our pieces of wood. Our hope is reborn and our faith is renewed, for our God is alive! Christ is risen! He is risen indeed!

Script: Hands meditation

Jesus himself stood among the apostles and said, 'Peace be with you.'

Let go of the stress... the worries... the in tray... the shopping lists... the things you know you have to do tomorrow... Jesus said, 'Peace be with you.'

As you breathe in now, imagine yourself breathing in that peace... 'Peace be with you.'

Then Jesus said, 'Why are you frightened?' Why... are... you... frightened?

Tell him about it now... the things that make you frightened

Then he said, 'Look at my hands and my feet.' Open your hands and look at them. Look at them carefully. Look at the different parts of your hands... the fingertips... the different lines on the palms... the back of your hands, with their joints and bones... the spots, the scars, the wrinkles and the bruises. Ask God to show you them as he sees them. Each one is unique throughout eternity and time. Unique. And loved...

Then turn your hands palm upwards, and look at the space between the palms and the wrist... the place where the nails went when Christ was crucified... the scars Jesus still carried even after he was raised from the dead... scars like red roses telling you of his love for you...

Jesus said, 'Look at my hands... Turn and look at someone else's hands, and let them show you theirs. Imagine that person is Jesus showing you his hands. Look at their hands... notice the differences between their hands and yours... think even of the softness of the hands... their vulnerability...

Open hands have no weapons in them. It is said that this is why people first began to shake hands as a greeting. 'Look! My hand is open. I have no knife in it. I come as a friend.' Christ comes as a friend.

Then Jesus said, 'Touch me and see...' Touch your hands onto the hands of the other person. Close your eyes... and feel the touching force... and the feeling of being touched... Imagine that it is Christ's hand you are touching. How might it feel to touch a real body that once was dead and now is alive? Christ is alive... real... touchable. But Christ's physical, real body has now returned to heaven. And he asks us to act as his body on earth till he returns...

Keep your eyes closed as you ponder the following words, spoken by Saint Teresa of Avila:

Christ has no body on earth but yours; no hands, no feet on earth but yours. Yours are the eyes through which he looks with compassion on the world; yours are the feet with which he walks to do good; yours are the hands with which he blessed all the world. Christ has no body now on the earth but yours.

No hands, no feet, on earth... but ours... to raise up the fallen.

No feet but ours... to seek the lost.

No eyes but ours... to see the silent tears of the suffering.

No ears but ours... to listen to the lonely.

No tongue but ours... to speak a word of comfort to the sad.

No heart but ours... to love the unloved.

Yours are the feet with which he walks to do good. Yours are the hands with which be blesses all the world. Yours are the hands... the feet... the eyes...

Your bodies are his body. Christ has no body now on earth but yours.

Script: Praying with Rublev

A

The angel of the Lord appears a number of times in the Old Testament... many interpret this as being Jesus. But in this story there are three mysterious angelic figures. Were they three angels? Were they Christ and two angels? Who are they?

They are also interpreted as prefiguring or symbolising the Trinity itself. Yet they cannot be the Trinity in all its glory – or Abraham would die for contemplating their majesty.

This picture was painted for an Orthodox Christian monastery. It is important to remember that because of the prohibition of images of God in the Ten Commandments, Orthodox Christians refuse to paint the Father. Jesus can be painted in their tradition because he has been made human and visible. You can only paint what has already been revealed. Yet God himself has said that we are allowed to portray angels. 'Make two cherubim out of hammered gold... ' says Exodus 25:18.

Here in this picture we have a revelation to Abraham being used symbolically to teach us something about God. This icon is using this mysterious story as a symbol to give a visual sermon about what God is like.

B

The figures in this icon are drawn within an invisible circle – symbolising eternity and the never-ending love of God. Within that circle there is a triangle formed by the heads of the three figures. A triangle within a circle is a traditional symbol of the Trinity.... a three-sided figure inside a one-sided figure... the three in one. For our God is three, and is also one...

The figures are seated, all reaching equal heights. No one in the Trinity is more important than the other...

In the centre of the table is a cup. Older pictures of this scene have a slaughtered animal in the cup. In this picture, what looks a little like a sacrificed lamb might also be a cup of wine. It is symbolising Christ's sacrifice for us and also reminding us of communion... not just the communion time when we eat the same bread and share the one cup, but also the communion and love at the centre of the Godhead...

Although Rublev never named these figures, traditionally the first figure on the left reminds us of God the Father; the second figure reminds us of the Son and the third reminds us of the Holy Spirit.

The figure on the left is dressed in gold or pink in some reproductions. Gold is often the colour of glory. For God is glorious...

The central figure is dressed as Jesus often is in icons... in purple and blue... the emperor's colours. For Christ is the ruler of all...

This figure, reminding us of Jesus, has a stripe on one shoulder which is reminiscent of a deacon's sash. Deacons in the Bible were appointed to serve others, to look after the widows and the orphans... so Jesus is one who rules as a servant king who looks after us...

His hands are extended towards the cup in blessing. Two fingers are extended – one for God, the other for humanity... reminding us that, in nature, Christ is both truly and fully God and yet also truly and fully human...

The figure on the right symbolises the Holy Spirit. This figure is dressed in green, the colour of new life... the colour of youth and strength... for the Spirit gives new life to us all. He is the Life-giver.

The three figures have wings, symbolising that they have flown in from above. They have come from heaven.

They are not of earth...

Each figure holds a staff, symbolising power. But the staffs are thin... they do not force that power on anyone. It is up to you to accept God's gentle and life-giving rule over you. Are you willing to do this?

Each staff points somewhere, but the picture is old and this is hard to see. The father figure points to a house, which on one level is Abraham's house. On another it is a reminder that, 'In my Father's house are many rooms... ' enough for everyone!

The central figure in purple points to a tree, which on one level is the oak at Mamre... on another level it is symbolic of the cross and of the tree of life which will heal the nations...

The third figure is pointing to a mountain which is very difficult to see. It is the mountain of spiritual experience, like Mount Sinai, where Moses saw the glory of God...

The three figures all seem to have the same face. As Jesus said, 'Anyone who has seen me has seen the Father.'

Looking at the three faces, each gaze leads you from one to the other, and then back around again. It is not easy to simply rest in one place when gazing at them. There is no clear beginning and no end to the figures, reminding us that God is eternal and timeless, without beginning or end...

Rublev manages to express the mystery of the Trinity in his image much better than many people can describe in words.

Look at the table. There is a space at this table. One side of it is empty... that space is for you... you are invited to come and share at the table... to meet God!

Script: Heaven's door

You are on holiday in Greece, and you are visiting the island of Patmos – the place where so long ago John the apostle had an amazing revelation.

You walk, admiring the sapphire sky and turquoise waters of the Aegean Sea, while the warm sea breeze is blowing gently across your face. Then, lying on the hillside in the shade of an olive tree, you close your eyes to pray... and something amazing happens.

In a bright and shining light you find yourself transported to the entrance of heaven itself... there is a door... but the door is padlocked, and the padlock is surrounded by huge chains... and, as if the chains weren't enough, there is a *no entry* sign fixed on it...

You stand by the padlocked door for a while, wondering why on earth you are here. You feel like you must be waiting for something... it seems as if there is nowhere else to go...

Suddenly someone appears... you somehow expected something spectacular...

Will it be an angel with many-coloured wings and a harp? Or Peter holding a bunch of golden keys? But no! It is a middle-aged man with a shaved head. He is dressed in a black suit, bow tie and long dark overcoat... reminding you of the type of person who stands outside pubs on a Friday night, to keep out the rowdier elements.

You ask him, 'Why is the door padlocked? Why am I here if I can't get inside? What is this all about?'

He replies, 'Beyond that door... the one swathed in chains... the one with the *no entry* sign... that is heaven. It is perfect... totally, totally perfect... there is nothing bad in there. No death... no pain... no selfishness... no conflict... nothing remotely evil. And you see, if we let you in... you'd spoil it... because you obviously aren't perfect. So *no entry*. Sorry.'

You reply, 'But, in that case, why am I here? Are you just showing me the door to make me feel bad? Isn't there anything I can do about it?'

'No. You'd have to transform into something else... someone perfect. It's as if you're a caterpillar and you need to be, well, more like a butterfly... and you can't possibly do that by yourself. So, no... you'll just have to stay here till the vision ends.'

And so you sit and wait... deeply disappointed and puzzled. For what is the point in having a vision... if all that happens is that you sit and wait by a door that you cannot open?

Then... you see a man coming. You hear groans... for he is dragging the most enormous set of bolt cutters that you have ever seen. They are as big as he is, and they weigh him down. Something in you wants to help him... but somehow... you know that this is a job that he has to do alone.

You look at him in amazement as he gets closer... he is covered in bruises... and his hands are bleeding. He takes the bolt cutters and he cuts the chains, one by one... and each chain that falls crashes to the ground, making the earth shake. Finally, he goes for the padlock. The other man, the one dressed like a bouncer, grabs his arm and is about to stop him opening the door, when the wounded man looks straight into his eyes. The bouncer looks terrified. He falls to his knees and says, 'My God! It's you.'

And something about the way he says it, makes you realise that he isn't swearing.

When he has recovered the power of speech, the man in black tries to phrase a question. But the words don't seem to come out very well. Every sentence ends in a mumble. But the wounded man takes him by the hand and explains, 'I know what you are trying to ask... how... and why?' He goes on... 'Well, there was only one way to get this door open. And I was the only one who could afford to buy the bolt cutters. Even though it cost me everything I had. But now... finally... the door can be opened.'

You look at the man once again, and you recognise him as the carpenter from Nazareth who preached peace and love... who talked of a kingdom where everyone who was at the bottom of the pile... everyone who was crushed and wounded... would be first... would be treated well. And now it looks like... finally... there will be a way into this wonderful place. For what would be the point of a kingdom where no one could get in?

You wonder if you are able to ask the man about what the bouncer said. For, of course, how can anyone step through the doors into somewhere completely perfect without ruining it?

Just as you are about to pluck up the courage to ask your question, the wounded carpenter looks straight into your eyes. It is a look that sees right into the depths of your soul... a look that rummages around inside the locked cupboards of your life... and looks into the secrets that you'd rather forget. You feel... vulnerable... you know you cannot hide anything... cannot lie... cannot run. But then you see him smile and you know that, despite all the skeletons in your cupboard, he is not going to reject you.

'Just watch,' he says... answering the question you weren't able to ask. 'You will understand.' And he takes the bolt cutters and does the most surprising thing of all. After cutting off the chains, he sets to work on the door itself. He lifts the heavy oak door off its hinges and throws it away as if it was as light as a feather. As it hits the ground, it smashes into a thousand splinters.

Then he himself stands in the doorway and says, 'No, you cannot enter without spoiling things. Yes, you still need to be transformed. And so the door itself needs to be replaced. I am the door. Enter through me, and you can be transformed. Perfection is impossible. I am capable of doing the impossible.'

And... as he stands in the doorway, he actually becomes the door. It's an open door... a door of such beauty your eyes fill with tears and your heart sings... you feel drawn inside with an almost magnetic pull... and yet you know that you still have the choice to walk away if you wish.

The black-suited man turns to you and says, 'You can go in now, if you like. But no one is forcing you. And you understand that if you step through this door, everything will be different. You will be transformed. Nothing can stay the same. You can still stay this side of the threshold if you want to.'

You pause... it seems to be a step that needs serious contemplation. Then you walk towards the door. You step through. You glimpse what lies beyond and you hear a voice say, 'After this I looked, and there before me was a door standing open in heaven... You are worthy, our Lord and God, to receive glory and honour and power, for you created all things, and by your will they were created and have their being.'

Script: The cross

Voice 1: We open our hands to be open to God who loves us and wants to draw close to us.

Voice 2: We open our hands, and look at our fingers... five fingers... for five precious wounds... two nails in his palms... two holes in his feet... a spear in his side... the sign of the cross is the sign of love.

Voice 3: Take your open right hand, palm down, and place it on your forehead.

Voice 1: In the name of the Father...

Voice 2: The creative mind who made all... who plans and longs for us to return and rest within his thoughts.

Voice 3: Now move your open right hand, palm down, and rest it on your heart.

Voice 1: In the name of the Son...

Voice 2: Jesus, whose heart beats with love... a heart both human and divine... the one who reached out in love and saved us...

Voice 3: And now take your open right hand, and place it on your left shoulder, in a minute moving it to your right shoulder when we say the word 'west'. At 'Amen', join your hands together.

Voice 1: In the name of the Holy Spirit...

Voice 2: Who gives life to the world from east to west... who gives gifts to the Church, and grows fruit in our hearts... who prays with us and through us... Amen.

Other books in the Multi-Sensory series

✳ **fresh** ✳ **innovative** ✳ **imaginative** ✳ **inspirational** ✳ **practical**

MULTI-SENSORY CHURCH

Over 30 ready-to-use ideas for creative churches and small groups

Sue Wallace

MULTI-SENSORY PRAYER

Over 60 ready-to-use ideas for creative churches and small groups

Sue Wallace

MULTI-SENSORY SCRIPTURE

50 innovative ideas for exploring the Bible in churches and small groups

Sue Wallace

MULTI-SENSORY TOGETHER

15 ready-to-use sessions for Bible exploration in creative small groups

Ian Birkinshaw

MULTI-SENSORY SEASONS

15 ready-to-use Bible-based sessions through the seasons for creative small groups

Wendy Rayner and Annie Slade

MULTI-SENSORY PARABLES

15 ready-to-use sessions on the stories Jesus told – for creative churches and small groups

Ian Birkinshaw

MULTI-SENSORY PROPHETS

15 ready-to-use sessions on God's messengers – for creative churches and small groups

Mike Law

MULTI-SENSORY MESSAGE

Ready-to-use Bible-based activities on mission – for creative churches and small groups.

Dave Maclure

MULTI-SENSORY WORLD

Global issues explored – for creative churches, youth groups and small groups

Craig Borlase

This series is just part of a wide range of resources for churches and small groups published by Scripture Union.

SU publications are available from Christian bookshops, on the Internet or via mail order. You can:

- phone SU's mail order line: 0845 0706006
- email info@scriptureunion.org.uk
- log on to www.scriptureunion.org.uk
- write to SU Mail Order, PO Box 5148, Milton Keynes MLO, MK2 2YX

wise traveller

Why doesn't happiness last?
How do I live with loss?
How can I make the most of
my relationships?

The *Wise Traveller* series offers
meditations for life's journey
to people who recognise that
life is not neat or painless, but
know that it is instead stuffed
full of meaning, mystery,
beauty and sacred encounters:

■ Original reflections, poems
and stories, and Christian
writings from across
history, offer pathways
for those seeking a more
authentic way of living.

■ A creative and open-
ended approach to biblical
spirituality and prayer.

■ An ideal gift for your
spiritually open friend,
relative, neighbour or
colleague.

■ Original reflections by
Multi-Sensory writer Sue
Wallace and others known
for their experimental
approach to Christian
spirituality including Steve
Hollinghurst, Martin Wroe
and Kester Brewin.

£2.99 each

TO ORDER:

Call SU Mail Order on **0845 0706006**
or visit **www.scriptureunion.org.uk**

SAVER OFFER: all 3 titles for the price of 2
(phone orders only, quoting code
MSWW09)

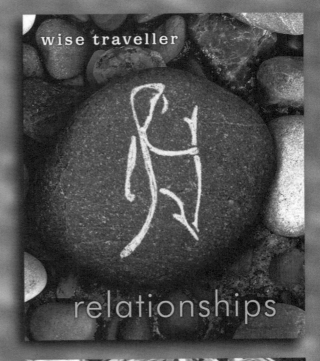